# Bid Better, Play Better:

## How to Think at the Bridge Table

## by Dorothy Hayden Truscott

PINNACLE BOOKS      LOS ANGELES

BID BETTER, PLAY BETTER

A new and revised Pinnacle Books edition, published by special
arrangement with the author and Harper & Row Publishers, Inc.

ISBN: 0-523-41265-7

First printing, December 1976
Second printing, October 1977
Third printing, May 1979
Fourth printing, June 1980

Printed in the United States of America

PINNACLE BOOKS, INC.
2029 Century Park East
Los Angeles, California 90067

To my children, without whom this book
would have been finished long ago

# Acknowledgment

Space and memory won't permit me to express my gratitude to all who have inspired me in this endeavor. I should like to thank in particular B. Jay Becker and Alan F. Truscott for reviewing the manuscript, Albert H. Morehead for his help with the history of bridge, and my father for his valuable suggestions and tireless editing.

# Contents

# Introduction

by B. JAY BECKER

There are all kinds of bridge books being published today but nearly all of them are more technical and less interesting than they should be, and few of them contain the sage advice and common sense you will encounter in this book.

A good bridge book should grip you in much the same way as a good detective story. You should feel the urge to read on even though your sense of comprehension is being taxed to the stretching point and you cannot quite integrate all the new thoughts you encounter.

What Dorothy Hayden does so effectively in this book is teach you how to think at the bridge table. There is not much point in asking you to memorize a series of general rules unless you understand the logic behind them. You cannot solve a difficult bridge problem by rote—the game is too complicated for that—but you can solve a great many problems if you appreciate the reason for a rule and know whether or not it applies to the particular situation confronting you.

There is an amazing similarity between the way Dorothy Hayden plays bridge and the way she wrote this book. We have been regular partners in tournaments for the past five years, and I am glad to say that during that time we have compiled a better record than any other pair in the country. Her clarity of thought at the bridge table is duplicated in her writing, and her exposition of Standard American bidding is an accurate reflection of how the leading experts in the United States play.

There are some chapters in this book which present old thoughts in new ways, and other chapters—especially with reference to defensive play and slam bidding—which expound new theories hitherto unpublished but nevertheless of extremely vital importance.

The style of bidding recommended is basically the simplest possible. Contrary to the philosophy of a handful of so-called "modern scientists," who employ innumerable artificial conventions and other specialized gadgets to describe certain types of hands, the methods advocated in this book are so natural and so logical that there is very little room left for partnership misunderstanding. These are the methods we have been using for the past several years, and they have stood up well against every type of competition we have encountered.

In our methods, if you bid diamonds, you are expected to have diamonds, and if you bid spades, you are expected to have spades. This may be regarded by some as a tedious and unadventurous way of playing bridge, but is at the same time, in our opinion, the most successful way of playing the game.

There are some hands and some illustrations, as well as some specialized conventions, referred to in this book which depart from so-called natural bidding, but they are the exception rather than the rule. After all, originality, ingenuity, and psychology also have an important place in bridge, and the ability to improvise when an unusual set of circumstances arises is a faculty whose use Dorothy Hayden would be the last one to discourage.

It may come as a surprise to some to learn that Mrs. Hayden is the only woman ever to have represented the United States in world championship play as a result of having qualified through the annual Trials method first instituted in 1961. Her performance in Buenos Aires in 1965 confirmed what many experts have known for a long time: that she is not only the best woman player in the world today, but that she can sit down in any company and more than hold her own.

Most players think that women do not have the stamina to meet the relentless and grueling requirements of the Trials or of national or world championship play, but I can testify firsthand that in Dorothy Hayden's case there is nothing to this contention. If she has a breaking point, I have yet to discover it. Her magnificent record in open events, as well as in mixed and women's events, is well known. But enough of this flattery of my favorite partner. I won't even mention her impeccably good manners, her fine sense of humor, her good looks, her status as one of the leading mathematicians in the bridge world, or anything else about her, because I know you must be waiting impatiently to read what Dorothy Hayden has to say about bridge.

# BID BETTER, PLAY BETTER

# 1

# The World of Bridge

It is estimated that there are forty million bridge players in the United States and Canada alone. How many of them realize that this game, which seems so modern, has a history of about five hundred years behind it?

The origin of playing cards themselves is obscure, but it is known that they were used in China as long ago as A.D. 969. It wasn't until three hundred years later that cards reached Europe. They first appeared in Venice, possibly introduced by Niccolo Polo and his son, Marco Polo, on their return from China. During the next century they spread rapidly throughout Europe and were well on time to catch the first boat to America. Legend tells us that Columbus's sailors threw their playing cards overboard in superstitious terror at the raging storms in the vast Atlantic. Later, on dry land, they regretted their rashness and made new ones out of leaves.

Playing cards arrived in England early in the fifteenth century, and it was here that the ancestor of modern bridge was born. This early game was called variously "triumph," "trump," "ruff and honours," "whisk and swabbers," and "whisk." English literature is full of references to the game. The earliest mention is 1529, but it is clear that it had been played long before that date.

By the seventeenth century the game, then known as "whisk" or "whist," was very popular in England. Just as today, the game was played by four people, the two sitting opposite each other being partners. Thirteen cards were dealt to each player, and the score was determined by the tricks won above and beyond the first six tricks, which eventually became known as the "book." There was also a bonus for honors, and two out of three games made a rubber. Unlike today, however, there was no bidding. Trump was determined by turning up the last card dealt. The player to the dealer's left always made the opening lead. The hand of dealer's partner was not exposed. The fact that all four hands were concealed made whist much more difficult than bridge. There were fewer experts and they were regarded with awe.

A great deal of betting went on in the coffee houses. Not only did the players bet among themselves, but standing around the table was a ring of kibitzers who were constantly making bets with the players as well as with one another. The procedure somewhat resembled a miniature stock exchange, and wagers were laid on anything from the play of a card to whether it would rain tomorrow. It was, in fact, a group of whist players at Edward Lloyd's Coffee House who in their spare time founded the famous Lloyd's of London.

Such was the lively atmosphere when Edmond Hoyle (1672–1769) arrived on the scene. A barrister of good family and education, Hoyle became the first professional whist instructor. He wrote the first book devoted to the game and it rapidly became a best seller, going through many editions. His section on probabilities is surprisingly modern, and much of what he wrote on card play and leading is still applicable. Before Hoyle's time, even such basic knowledge as the art of finessing was understood mainly by experts and those in contact with experts. Now it was available to all. As a result, the popularity of the game grew by leaps and bounds, particularly among the ladies and gentlemen of society. Whist became a highly respected intellectual pursuit. Hoyle established the tradition of law and order in card play, and the expression "according to Hoyle" became part of the English language.

Perhaps the most famous hand in the entire history of

bridge is the one said to have been dealt about two hundred years ago in the gaming rooms at Bath, England, to a Duke of Cumberland, probably the son of King George III. The Duke held the West hand in the diagram and, incredible though it may appear, he never took a single trick!

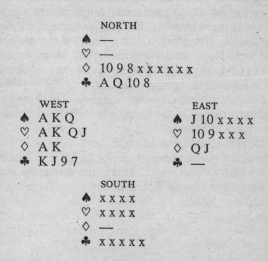

```
                    NORTH
                 ♠ —
                 ♡ —
                 ◇ 10 9 8 x x x x x x
                 ♣ A Q 10 8

        WEST                      EAST
     ♠ A K Q                   ♠ J 10 x x x x
     ♡ A K Q J                 ♡ 10 9 x x x
     ◇ A K                     ◇ Q J
     ♣ K J 9 7                 ♣ —

                    SOUTH
                 ♠ x x x x
                 ♡ x x x x
                 ◇ —
                 ♣ x x x x x
```

Clubs were trumps, and the Duke had the opening lead. In an effort to draw trumps as quickly as possible, he led the club seven. North won with the eight and led a diamond for South to ruff. South returned a trump, West played the nine, and North won with the ten. Another diamond ruff put South in again to lead his last trump. North won, drew the Duke's last trump, and claimed the balance with his seven established diamond winners.

On this hand, the Duke of Cumberland lost twenty thousand pounds, the equivalent today of much more than half a million dollars. Of course the Duke was swindled. This hand was used by hustlers of the eighteenth and nineteenth centuries to take advantage of the betting habits of the day. The actual hand can be found in one of Hoyle's editions published long before the Duke's disaster.

From England, whist soon spread throughout most of Europe and the United States. No history of the game, however short, should fail to mention the famous French whist expert, Guillaume Deschapelles (1780–1847). He is described by his contemporary James Clay, the English whist authority, as the finest whist player "beyond comparison the world has ever seen." Soldiering in one of the wars of his time, Deschapelles lost his right hand, severed at the wrist. Nevertheless, he continued to play whist, chess, and, more remarkably, billiards. Many bridge experts have been good chess players, and many chess experts have been good bridge players. But no one has ever excelled at *both* so outstandingly as Deschapelles. He was acknowledged as the finest whist player *and* the finest chess player of his day.

Although he contributed much to the science of whist, Deschapelles is remembered chiefly as the inventor of the coup which bears his name. This is the deliberate sacrifice of a high unsupported honor in order to force an entry into partner's hand.

Example.

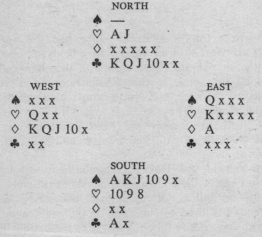

NORTH
♠ —
♡ A J
◇ x x x x x
♣ K Q J 10 x x

WEST
♠ x x x
♡ Q x x
◇ K Q J 10 x
♣ x x

EAST
♠ Q x x x
♡ K x x x x
◇ A
♣ x x x

SOUTH
♠ A K J 10 9 x
♡ 10 9 8
◇ x x
♣ A x

Against a contract of four spades, West leads the diamond king, won perforce by the ace. What should East return at trick two? The only return to beat the contract is the king of hearts, a Deschapelles coup. With any other return, West can never get in to cash his diamond winner.

The next great name to appear on the whist scene is that of Henry Jones (1831–1899) of London, better known by his pseudonym of "Cavendish." Author of many books on the game, he had more influence on the world of whist than any writer since Hoyle. Among his contributions to the science of the game was his system of leads. One of them, the lead of the fourth best, has remained standard to this day. Duplicate players may be surprised to learn that the first duplicate tournament was directed by Cavendish in London in 1857, more than one hundred years ago.

Toward the end of the nineteenth century, a variation of whist was introduced. It was called "bridge," but is now referred to as "bridge whist" to avoid confusion.

There were several differences between whist and bridge. Instead of turning up the last card to determine the trump suit, the dealer was allowed to choose the trump suit or no-trump if he desired. He also had the option of passing the decision to his partner. The opponents were allowed to double, and the dealer's side could redouble. An infinite number of doubles and redoubles was permitted, which introduced an undesirable gambling element into the by now staid game of whist. In keeping with the courtesy of the age, the opening leader was required to ask, "Partner, may I lead?" Whereupon, partner, if he didn't plan to double, was required to respond, "Pray do." Another difference was that in bridge the dummy was exposed. This made the play of the cards much more scientific, and whist authorities actually recommended bridge to their pupils as an aid to learning how to play whist.

About 1904, the element of competitive bidding was introduced. Instead of the dealer or his partner being allowed to name the trump suit, all four players could bid in turn as high as they chose for the privilege of naming trumps. This new form of the game, known as "auction bridge," quickly supplanted bridge whist. The parent game

5

whist, however, continued to be played side by side with auction.

About 1918, another variation of bridge, called "plafond," became popular in France. The chief new feature was the concept of counting toward game only those tricks that were contracted for in the auction.

In 1925–26, Harold S. Vanderbilt, a member of one of the wealthiest and most famous American families, combined the best features of auction bridge and plafond with a new scoring system, including the new idea of vulnerability, and called it "contract bridge." Thanks to Vanderbilt's social position and tremendous reputation in the bridge world, as well as his perfectly balanced scoring system, contract bridge was immediately accepted. It soon eclipsed all other forms of the game.

The credit for making contract bridge an international success must go to the dynamic Ely Culbertson (1891–1955). Expert player, author of an enormous number of bridge texts, founder of *Bridge World Magazine*, and organizer of many bridge activities, Culbertson was the outstanding personality and world-wide authority in the early years of contract.

## The World of Bridge Today

In this country, duplicate tournaments had been conducted since 1891 by the American Whist League. (Bridge, for some reason, was not considered suitable for duplicate at first.) In 1927, the American Auction Bridge League was formed. It soon became the American Bridge League, dropping the word "auction" so as to include contract bridge as well. In 1937, this group merged with other existing organizations, and the tournament bridge world was finally united under the auspices of the American Contract Bridge League.

The A.C.B.L. today conducts three national tournaments annually. It also sanctions about forty regional and four hundred sectional tournaments each year throughout the country. The league has over five thousand affiliated bridge clubs, each of which holds from one to fourteen duplicate games a week.

All tournament players are rated by "master points," which are awarded for performances at all levels. Winning a club duplicate is worth a fraction of a point, depending on the number of tables in play. Winning the National Blue Ribbon Pairs is worth 125 points. The A.C.B.L. keeps track of all master points won by members and ranks the players accordingly. Anyone with 300 points (of which at least 50 have been won at the regional or national level) is a Life Master, and there are now over twenty-six thousand Life Masters. Charles H. Goren, the successor to Ely Culbertson as the world's foremost bridge authority, held the top spot on the master-point list from 1944 to 1962, when he was overtaken by Oswald Jacoby. The present leader, with a commanding margin over his nearest rivals, is Hollywood television producer Barry Crane.

The A.C.B.L. also distributes free to its members a monthly magazine of about 90 pages called *The Bulletin*. It keeps everyone up to date on what's going on in the world of bridge.

The tremendous growth of the A.C.B.L. is astounding. (Membership costs $6 a year and players usually join through their local A.C.B.L. affiliated club.) In 1937 the League had about 5,000 members. By 1950 there were 20,000 members. In 1960 the 100,000 mark was passed. As this is being written, there are 200,000 members, with no apparent end in sight to the phenomenal expansion.

International bridge competitions are held annually under the direction of the World Bridge Federation. The six players who form the North American team are chosen each year as follows: The teams winning the four major national team titles, the Vanderbilt, the Spingold, the Reisinger, and the Grand National take part in play-off matches with a semi-final and a final stage.

About 50 countries belong to the World Bridge Federation. The World Team Championship has been dominated by the Italians, who have won 16 times in a 20-year period. Their closest rivals have been the United States, Great Britain, and France, with Canada, Australia, Brazil, and Taiwan not far behind. On the women's scene international honors have been shared between the United States, Italy, Great Britain, South Africa, and Sweden.

Tomorrow when you sit down at the card table, remember that you are part of this huge world of bridge. And just as the wonders of atomic science today are built on generations of research and experiment by the scientists of yesterday, so the game of bridge today is a better game thanks to the cumulative contributions of the experts of the past.

## What System Do You Play?

The vast majority of bridge players in this country use Standard American bidding which was called Culbertson in the thirties and Goren in the fifties. Culbertson played a major role in formulating what is now Standard American, and Goren did a tremendous job of teaching it to the public. But whether you call it Culbertson, Goren, or Standard American, it is one and the same system.

Many writers on bridge try to sell the reader a new system of bidding. Each assures him that if he adopts the new system he will always get the utmost out of each hand, will win more rubbers, will win more tournaments.

I have no new bidding system to offer and I seriously doubt that a new system ever made a good bidder out of a poor one. Furthermore, from the standpoint of all-around efficiency combined with simplicity, I'm firmly convinced that Standard American has yet to be equalled.

The way to improve your bridge is not to change your system but to cut down on your mistakes. A player who averages twenty errors a session in the bidding and play of the various hands he encounters is twice as good as one who averages forty errors a session.

Naturally it's impossible to cut out all mistakes. The expert hasn't been born who doesn't make some. I'd say that any player who averages less than two mistakes a session deserves the title of expert. (Of course in this rarefied atmosphere I'm counting even such minute errors as the play of the three spot when the four would have been better.) The average player probably makes about one hundred mistakes in bidding and play during an afternoon of bridge. Fortunately for his self-esteem, he usually will recognize only about 10 percent of them.

The immediate goal of every player should be to reduce the number of his mistakes, just as a golfer strives to cut down on the number of poor shots he makes in every round. Even the top bridge players are constantly trying to make fewer mistakes. They *must* if they are going to excel in major tournaments or international matches. Remember, the United States team has only won three world titles since 1954, beating the great Italian Blue Team exactly once. We might have won them all if our players had made fewer mistakes!

There are two main causes of error in bridge: bad judgment and ignorance. Errors in judgment are not easy to correct, but errors due to ignorance are.

Many bidding errors occur because the player doesn't thoroughly understand the system he is playing.

Standard American is basically a *natural* system of bidding. By natural, I mean that if a player bids spades, he has spades. If he bids diamonds, he has diamonds, and so on. In direct contrast, there are many One Club systems, such as Precision, Blue Team, Schenken, and Roman, which may be very artificial. There is even a system in which all opening bids are weak and a pass is strong!

Of course there are many artificial conventions which can be tacked onto Standard American (see Chapter 11). For example, just because a pair use weak two-bids, or Landy or Texas, doesn't mean they aren't playing Standard American. It just means they have added some gadgets. For each gadget you add, however, you must give up some natural bid. As everyone knows, if you use Blackwood, you're often unable to use the bid of four no-trump in its natural meaning. Furthermore, the more gadgets you use, the greater the risk of partnership misunderstanding. As you've probably realized by now, I'm a firm believer in natural bidding. But, there are two artificial conventions, Blackwood and Stayman, that are so widely used they've

9

become an integral part of Standard American. These and other conventions will be discussed in Chapter 11.

There are two important guideposts which distinguish one *natural* bidding system from another: the forcing principle and the no-trump structure. Thus a foreign expert, familiar with another natural system such as Acol (the most popular bidding system in Great Britain), would have only two vital questions to ask before sitting down to play Standard American: "What bids are forcing?" and "What do the no-trump bids mean?" These two subjects will be discussed first.

# 2

# Forcing Bids

It's hard to overemphasize the importance of forcing bids. They're as vital to bridge players as traffic lights are to drivers of motor vehicles. If a driver didn't know that red meant "stop," green meant "go," and amber meant "caution," chaos and manslaughter would be the result. So it is in bidding at the bridge table. The different kinds of forcing and nonforcing bids are the traffic signals of the partnership. If one partner is ignorant of their meaning, chaos will often follow, and attempted manslaughter shouldn't be ruled out.

Many bidding mistakes occur simply because a player doesn't know whether or not a certain bid is forcing. Most textbooks are prepared for beginners, and the author is obliged to concentrate on such problems as when or how to open the bidding, when to respond, etc. Only casually throughout the book can he refer to the fact that a certain bid is forcing. If a reader wishes to brush up on the subject of forcing bids, he often has to hunt through the entire book in order to pick out the forcing principles. Even then he may have trouble organizing them in his mind, because some appear to be contradictory.

Since this is not a text for beginners, let's plunge right into a discussion of this most important concept.

There are actually two kinds of forcing bids: those which are forcing for one round only, and those which are

11

forcing to game. If a bid is forcing for one round only, partner is required to keep the bidding open once. If a bid is forcing to game, *both* members of the partnership are obliged to continue bidding until game is reached or until the opponents are doubled.

The principles that cover the standard forcing situations are:

*Principle* 1.     An opening two-bid in a suit is forcing to game. No other opening bid is forcing. (But see Chapter 11 for Weak Two-Bids.)

Example:
SOUTH       NORTH
 2 ♠

Both North and South must continue to game.

*Principle* 2.     A jump shift (jump in a new suit) by either partner of the side that opens the bidding is forcing to game.

Example 1.
SOUTH       NORTH
 1 ◇          1 ♡
 2 ♠

South's bid of two spades is forcing to game. Note that when responder has bid at the one level, the only bid which opener can make that cannot be passed is a jump shift.

Example 2.
SOUTH       NORTH
 1 ◇          2 ♡

A jump shift by responder is not only forcing to game. It is an invitation to slam.

*Principle* 3.     A new suit by responder is forcing for one round.

Example:

| SOUTH | NORTH |
|-------|-------|
| 1 ◇ | 1 ♠ |

South must bid once more.

*Principle* 4.     Any jump bid by responder is forcing to game.

Example:

| SOUTH | NORTH |
|-------|-------|
| 1 ♠ | 3 ♠ |

Both North and South must continue to game.

*Principle* 5.     A jump bid by opener (except a jump shift) is not forcing, although it is very encouraging.

Example:

| SOUTH | NORTH |
|-------|-------|
| 1 ◇ | 1 ♡ |
| 3 ♡ | |

North may pass with a minimum.

Exception: If responder has bid at the two level, a jump by opener is forcing to game.

Example:

| SOUTH | NORTH |
|-------|-------|
| 1 ♡ | 2 ♣ |
| 3 ♡ | |

This situation is forcing to game. North can't have a minimum because he bid at the two level. The combined values of the hands must add up to game.

*Principle* 6.     Once a suit has been agreed upon, a bid in another suit is forcing for one round.

Example:

| SOUTH | NORTH |
|-------|-------|
| 1 ♠   | 2 ♠   |
| 3 ♡   |       |

North must make another bid. With a minimum hand he should simply rebid three spades. With other than a minimum he may bid three no-trump, four clubs, four diamonds, four hearts, or four spades, depending on which bid best describes his hand.

*Principle 7.* A bid in the opponent's suit, called a cue-bid, is artificial and forcing. It will nearly always lead to a game or even a slam. (For examples see Chapter on Advanced Bidding.)

Example:

| SOUTH | WEST |
|-------|------|
| 1 ♡   | 2 ♡  |

East and West are committed to game. West may hold something like:
♠ A Q J x    ♡ —    ◇ K Q 9 x x    ♣ A Q J x

*Principle 8.* A new suit or jump by responder is not forcing if he has previously passed.

Example:

| SOUTH | NORTH |
|-------|-------|
| Pass  | 1 ♡   |
| 3 ♡   |       |

North may pass with a minimum because he knows South has less than an opening bid.

Exception: Over an opening bid of one no-trump, a jump by responder is still forcing to game even though he has previously passed.

Example:

| SOUTH | NORTH |
|-------|-------|
| Pass  | 1 NT  |
| 3 ♠   |       |

This sequence is forcing to game. Even though South is a passed hand, he can easily hold enough to insist on game opposite an opening bid of one no-trump.

*Principle* 9.     A reverse (a rebid at the level of two or more in a higher-ranking suit than the one originally named) is a very powerful bid because it requires partner to give a preference at the three level. It is highly invitational but not forcing.

Example:

| SOUTH | NORTH |
|-------|-------|
| 1 ♦   | 1 ♠   |
| 2 ♥   |       |

North may only pass with a dead minimum, such as ♠ K J x x x ♡ J x x ◇ x x ♣ x x x. If his red suits were interchanged, however, he should naturally give partner a preference to three diamonds. He should expect South to hold a hand like ♠ Q x ♡ A K 10 x ◇ A K 10 x x x ♣ x.

*Principle.* 10.     A new suit bid by responder is not forcing if the opener has just bid one no-trump.

Example 1.

| SOUTH | NORTH |
|-------|-------|
| 1 NT  | 2 ♥   |

North's bid of two hearts is a "sign-off." South must pass. (Two clubs, however, would be Stayman, which will be discussed in Chapter 11.)

Example 2.

| SOUTH | NORTH |
|-------|-------|
| 1 ◊   | 1 ♠   |
| 1 NT  | 2 ♡   |

South will pass if he has longer hearts than spades, and otherwise correct to two spades.

*Principle* 11.    If the opponents have opened the bidding, jump bids invite game but are not forcing.

Example 1.

| EAST | SOUTH | WEST | NORTH |
|------|-------|------|-------|
| 1 ♣  | 1 ♡   | Pass | 2 NT  |

South will pass if he has a minimum overcall and a relatively balanced hand.

Example 2.

| EAST | SOUTH | WEST | NORTH |
|------|-------|------|-------|
| 1 ♣  | Dbl.  | Pass | 2 ♡   |

South will pass if he has a minimum take-out double.

*Principle* 12.    Any suit response to an opening bid of two no-trump is forcing.

Example:

| SOUTH | NORTH |
|-------|-------|
| 2 NT  | 3 ◊   |

South must bid again.

*Principle* 13.    A bid by the opposition may relieve a player from his obligation to bid.

Example:

| SOUTH | WEST | NORTH | EAST |
|-------|------|-------|------|
| 1 ♡   | Pass | 1 ♠   | 2 ♣  |

16

South may pass with a minimum hand because East's bid of two clubs has kept the bidding open for North.

*Principle* 14.     When a part score is held, a new suit or a jump by responder is not forcing if it completes the partial. A jump shift, however, is still forcing.

Example 1.

| SOUTH | NORTH | (North-South have 60 on score.) |
|-------|-------|-------|
| 1 ♠ | 2 ♡ | |

South may pass.

Example 2.

| SOUTH | NORTH | (North-South have 60 on score.) |
|-------|-------|-------|
| 1 ♠ | 3 ◊ | |

South must bid again despite the part score.

Now let's test your knowledge of forcing bids.


## QUIZ ON FORCING BIDS

In the following bidding sequences it's your turn to bid at the question mark. If you could possibly pass, put a check mark in the column headed NF to show that the sequence is nonforcing. If you are obliged to make one more bid, put a check in the column headed F for "forcing." And if both you and your partner must continue bidding until game is reached (or until opponents have been doubled), put a check in the column headed GF for "game forcing." Then check your answers against those shown on page 19 and rate yourself according to the scale.

| 1. | SOUTH | NORTH | NF | F | GF |
|----|-------|-------|----|----|----|
| | 1 ♣ | ? | ✓ | — | — |

17

| | | | NF | F | GF |
|---|---|---|---|---|---|
| 2. | SOUTH<br>1 ♣<br>1 ♡<br>? | NORTH<br>1 ◇<br>1 ♠ | — | ✓ | — |
| 3. | SOUTH<br>1 ♡<br>3 ♠ | NORTH<br>1 ♠<br>? | ✓ | — | — |
| 4. | SOUTH<br>1 NT<br>? | NORTH<br>2 ♠ | ✓ | — | — |
| 5. | SOUTH<br>1 ◇<br>1 ♠<br>? | NORTH<br>1 ♡<br>2 NT | — | — | ✓ |
| 6. | SOUTH<br>3 ◇<br>? | NORTH<br>3 ♠ | — | — | ✓ |
| 7. | SOUTH<br>1 ♡<br>3 ♣ | NORTH<br>2 ♡<br>? | — | ✓ | — |
| 8. | SOUTH<br>1 ♠<br>2 ♠ | NORTH<br>2 ♣<br>? | ✓ | — | — |
| 9. | SOUTH<br>1 ◇<br>2 ♣ | NORTH<br>1 ♡<br>? | ✓ | — | — |
| 10. | SOUTH<br>1 ♣<br>2 ◇ | NORTH<br>1 ♡<br>? | ✓ | ✓ | — |
| 11. | SOUTH<br>2 NT | NORTH<br>? | — | ✓ | — |

| 12. | SOUTH | NORTH | NF | F | GF |
|-----|-------|-------|-----|-----|-----|
|     | Pass  | 1 ♡   |     |     |     |
|     | 2 NT  | ?     | —   | ✓   | —   |

| 13. | SOUTH | NORTH | NF | F | GF |
|-----|-------|-------|-----|-----|-----|
|     | Pass  | 1 NT  |     |     |     |
|     | 3 ◇   | ?     | —   | —   | ✓   |

| 14. | SOUTH | NORTH | NF | F | GF |
|-----|-------|-------|-----|-----|-----|
|     | 2 ♠   | 2 NT  |     |     |     |
|     | 3 ♠   | ?     | ✓   | —   | —   |

| 15. | SOUTH | NORTH | NF | F | GF |
|-----|-------|-------|-----|-----|-----|
|     | 1 ♡   | 1 NT  |     |     |     |
|     | 3 ♡   | ?     | ✓   | —   | —   |

| 16. | SOUTH | NORTH | NF | F | GF |
|-----|-------|-------|-----|-----|-----|
|     | 1 ♣   | 1 ♡   |     |     |     |
|     | 1 NT  | 2 ◇   |     |     |     |
|     | ?     |       | ✓   | —   | —   |

## Answers to Quiz

1. NF. Principle 1. The only opening bid which is forcing is an opening two-bid in a suit.
2. F. Principle 3. Any new suit by responder is forcing for one round.
3. NF. Principle 5. A jump by opener is strong but not forcing.
4. NF. Principle 10. South is expected to pass.
5. GF. Principle 4. Any jump by responder is forcing to game.
6. F. Principle 3. A new suit by responder is forcing for one round.
7. F. Principle 6. When a suit has been agreed upon, a bid in another suit is forcing for one round.
8. NF. North will usually bid again, but he should pass with a dead minimum, such as ♠ x x ♡ J x x ◇ x x ♣ A Q J x x x.

9. NF. A new suit by opener is not forcing. It may be a minimum opening bid.
10. NF. Principle 9. North should rarely pass, however, because the reverse marks South with a very strong hand although not quite enough to make a forcing jump shift.
11. NF. Principle 1. The bid of two in a suit is the only opening bid that is forcing.
12. NF. Principle 8. A jump by a passed hand is not forcing.
13. GF. Principle 8. Exception. After an opening bid of one no-trump, a jump response is always forcing to game.
14. GF. Principle 1. An opening bid of two in a suit is forcing all the way to game.
15. NF. Principle 5. A jump by opener is not forcing.
16. NF. Principle 11. A new suit by responder after a rebid of one no-trump by opener is not forcing.

RATE YOURSELF AS FOLLOWS:

| | |
|---|---|
| No mistakes .............. | Expert! |
| 1 or 2 mistakes ........... | Very good |
| 3 or 4 mistakes ........... | Above average |
| 5 or 6 mistakes ........... | Average |
| 7 or more mistakes ........ | Well, why not just reread this chapter and try the Quiz again? |

# The No-Trump Structure

## PART I. Opening Bids of One, Two, and Three No-Trump and Their Responses

The backbone of any bidding system is its no-trump structure. In order to determine the number of tricks you and your partner can take at no-trump, a point-count method of evaluating honors is useful. The one devised by Milton Work and made popular by Charles Goren is by far the most widely used today because of its simplicity:

> The ace counts *4 points*.
> The king counts *3 points*.
> The queen counts *2 points*.
> The jack counts *1 point*.

It's obvious that with the above 4–3–2–1 point count there are a total of 40 points in the deck.

Thirty-seven points between your hand and partner's should produce a grand slam in no-trump. For example: four aces, four kings, four queens, and one jack (37 points) should add up to thirteen tricks. If it can be determined that a partnership has 37 points, there can be no ace missing so there's no need to use Blackwood before bidding seven no-trump.

Of course it's possible to lay out 37 points between the two hands in such a way that thirteen tricks can't be made. However, the odds favor bidding a grand slam with 37 or more points. Similarly, the odds favor bidding a small slam with 33 or more points. A game at no-trump should be undertaken with 26 or more points.

> Seven no-trump: 37 points
> Six no-trump:    33 points
> Three no-trump: 26 points

Naturally to open with a bid of no-trump you need balanced distribution. Otherwise your hand would be more valuable in a suit contract. The ideal distribution for no-trump are 4–4–3–2, 4–3–3–3, and 5–3–3–2. *Never open no-trump with a singleton or a void.*

I'm frequently asked whether it's proper to open no-trump with a five-card major. The answer is yes if the rest of the hand is suitable. It's better to open a hand such as ♠ A Q ♡ K J 9 x x ◇ K J x ♣ K x x with one no-trump rather than one heart because of the rebid problem.

### Standard American Requirements For Opening Bids of One, Two, or Three No-Trump

Important note: A player with a five-card suit who is opening no-trump at any level or raising no-trump to any level can regard his long suit as the equivalent of one high-card point.

*One no-trump: 16 to 18 points* and balanced distribution. Example:

♠ A K x   ♡ K J 9   ◇ K Q x x   ♣ J x x

*Two no-trump: 21 to 23 points* and balanced distribution. Example:

♠ A Q x   ♡ K Q x x   ◇ A J   ♣ K Q J x

*Three no-trump: 24–26 points* and balanced distribution. Example:

♠ A K J   ♡ K Q J x   ◇ A Q J   ♣ K J x.

Because of these precise values, no-trump bidding has become a relatively exact science.

22

NOTE: Many players tend to avoid these no-trump bids if they have a weak suit, especially if it is a weak doubleton. But the consensus of modern expert opinion is that the bid should be made in spite of the obvious danger that such a weakness represents. Choosing another bid creates rebid problems, and the distortion often leads the partnership to the wrong contract.

These ranges change slightly, with increased accuracy, if weak two-bids are used. (See Chapter 11.) Two no-trump opening bids are made with 21 or 22 points. Two clubs followed by two no-trump shows 23 or 24. The range for three no-trump narrows to 25–26, and slightly better hands, with 27 or 28 points, can bid two clubs followed by a jump to three no-trump. Notice that the delayed two no-trump and three no-trump bids always show better hands than the same bids made directly.

## Responding to an Opening Bid of One No-Trump When You Have a Balanced Hand

Add your points to partner's known total of 16 to 18, and keep in mind those three milestones:

> 26 points *are needed for game.*
> 33 points *are needed for a small slam.*
> 37 points *are needed for a grand slam.*

Therefore:

> *With 0 to 7 points*, pass. Game is remote.
> *With 8 or 9 points*, bid two no-trump. Partner will pass with 16 points and bid game with 17 or 18.
> *With 10 to 14 points*, bid three no-trump.
> *With 15 or 16 points,* bid four no-trump. Partner will pass with 16 points and carry on with more.
> NOTE: Four no-trump is not Blackwood when it's a direct raise of partner's no-trump bid. Furthermore, it's usually unnecessary to check for aces when bidding a slam at no-trump. With 33 points you can't be missing two aces.
> *With 17 or 18 points*, bid six no-trump

*With 19 or 20 points,* bid five no-trump. This is stronger than a raise to six no-trump and invites seven no-trump. Obviously it is forcing.

*With 21 or more points,* sit right up and bid seven no-trump!


## Responding to an Opening Bid of One No-Trump When You Have an Unbalanced Hand

*With a weak hand,* either pass or bid two spades, two hearts, or two diamonds. (Two clubs in response to one no-trump is an artificial bid and will be discussed in Chapter 11.)

Example:
Partner opens one no-trump. You hold ♠ Q J x x x x ♡ x x x ◇ x ♣ x x x. Respond two spades. This is a sign-off bid and partner is expected to pass.

*With a good hand and a five card major,* bid three of the major. This gives partner three choices. 1. With a doubleton in your suit he'll return to three no-trump. 2. With three or more in your suit, he'll raise you to game. 3. With a super-duper fit in your suit and key cards (aces and kings) he may "cue" bid an ace on the way in case you're interested in slam.

Example 1.

| PARTNER | YOU |
|---|---|
| ♠ K x | ♠ A Q 10 x x |
| ♡ A Q x x | ♡ x x |
| ◇ K J x x | ◇ Q x x |
| ♣ K 10 x | ♣ Q J x |

The bidding:

| | |
|---|---|
| 1 NT | 3 ♠ |
| 3 NT | Pass |

Your bid of three spades is forcing to game and shows five or more spades. Partner holds only two spades so he returns to three no-trump.

Example 2.

| PARTNER | YOU |
|---------|-----|
| ♠ A x | ♠ x x |
| ♡ Q 10 x | ♡ A J 9 x x |
| ◇ A J 10 x | ◇ K Q x x |
| ♣ K Q x x | ♣ x x |

The bidding:

| | |
|---|---|
| 1 NT | 3 ♡ |
| 4 ♡ | Pass |

This time partner has three trumps for you so he raises to game in hearts. (A combined holding of eight cards makes a good trump suit.)

Example 3.

| PARTNER | YOU |
|---------|-----|
| ♠ K J x x | ♠ A Q 10 x x |
| ♡ A x | ♡ x x x |
| ◇ A 10 x | ◇ Q x x |
| ♣ A J 10 x | ♣ Q x |

The bidding:

| | |
|---|---|
| 1 NT | 3 ♠ |
| 4 ♣ | 4 ♠ |
| Pass | |

Here partner bids four clubs over your three spades to show an exceptionally fine hand in support of spades and, incidentally, the ace of clubs. Unfortunately you don't have enough to accept the slam invitation and sign off at four spades.

*With six or more cards in a major suit and a fair hand,* jump to four spades or four hearts.

Example:
You hold   ♠ x   ♡ K J 9 x x x x   ◇ Q x x   ♣ x x.

Over partner's opening bid of one no-trump, jump to four hearts. Partner must pass. NOTE: With a seven-card suit, very few high-card points are needed for game when partner has opened one no-trump.

*With a strong hand and a possibility of slam,* jump to three of your suit and re-evaluate the partnership potential after hearing partner's rebid.

Example:

| PARTNER | YOU |
|---------|-----|
| ♠ K x x x | ♠ A J 10 x x |
| ♡ K x | ♡ A J x |
| ◇ A J x | ◇ x |
| ♣ A Q x x | ♣ K x x x |

The bidding:

| | |
|------|------|
| 1 NT | 3 ♠ |
| 4 ♣ | 6 ♠ |
| Pass | |

A sound opening bid opposite an opening one no-trump will produce a slam if a trump fit can be established. When partner rebids four clubs he shows an excellent spade fit including the club ace. This is all you need to know to undertake six spades.

### Responding to an Opening Bid of Two No-Trump When You Have a Balanced Hand

When your partner opens two no-trump he could hold 21, 22, or 23 points. These different point-count holdings do not occur with equal frequency, however. The vast majority of times he'll have 21 or 22 points. A 23-point hand·has the lowest frequency. Therefore when partner opens two no-trump be realistic and don't expect him to have more than 22 points.

*With 0 to 3 points,* pass. Game is remote.
*With 4 to 9 points,* raise to three no-trump.
*With 10 or 11 points,* jump to four no-trump, inviting six no-trump. Partner will pass with a minimum and carry on to six no-trump with a maximum.

*With 12 or 13 points*, bid six no-trump directly.

*With 14 or 15 points*, bid five no-trump. This is stronger than a raise to six no-trump and invites seven no-trump. Obviously it is forcing.

*With 16 or more points*, bid seven no-trump.

Remember that in all these raises a five-card suit is the equivalent of a point.


## Responding to an Opening Bid of Two No-Trump When You Hold an Unbalanced Hand

In each of the following examples partner has opened with a bid of two no-trump:

Example 1.
You hold ♠ x ♡ Q x x x x x ◇ x x ♣ x x x x.

Bid three hearts. This is a forcing bid and partner will probably rebid three no-trump. Now you will bid four hearts, which is where the hand belongs.

Example 2.
You hold ♠ x ♡ K J x x x ◇ K x ♣ x x x x.

Bid four hearts directly over two no-trump. This is a mild slam try. Partner will re-evaluate his hand with hearts in mind as a trump suit. With good hearts support and control cards (aces and kings), he may carry on.

Example 3.
You hold ♠ x x ♡ K J x x x ◇ K x x ♣ x x x.

Bid three hearts and allow partner to choose the final contract of three no-trump or four hearts.

Example 4.
You hold ♠ x ♡ x x x ◇ J x x x x ♣ x x x.

Pass. An eleven-trick game in diamonds is out of the question. Unfortunately, there's no way to stop the bidding at three diamonds, which is where the hand belongs. So, pass and take a small licking at two no-trump undoubled. If you should be fortunate enough to be doubled, you could then retreat to three diamonds, which would no longer be forcing.

Example 5.
You hold ♠ A 10 9 x x  ♡ A J 10 x x  ◇ x x  ♣ x.

This is a slam hand. Bid three spades. If partner raises to four spades, jump to six spades. If partner rebids three no-trump, jump to six hearts. Partner is bound to have good support for one of your suits.

## Responding to an Opening Bid of Three No-Trump When You Have a Balanced Hand

Hands with 24, 25, and 26 points are so rare you can play bridge regularly for a year without holding an opening three no-trump bid. If partner should open three no-trump, however, play him for 25 points.

*With 0 to 6 points*, pass.

*With 7 or 8 points*, raise to four no-trump, inviting six no-trump. Partner will pass with a minimum and continue with a maximum.

*With 9 or 10 points*, bid six no-trump.

*With 11 or 12 points*, bid five no-trump, inviting seven no-trump. This is forcing.

*With 13 or more points*, bid seven no-trump.

## Responding to an Opening Bid of Three No-Trump When You Have an Unbalanced Hand

Any good six-card suit will produce a slam.

Example:
You hold  ♠ x  ♡ A Q 10 9 x x  ◇ x x x  ♣ x x x.

Jump to six hearts.

Summing up: To open the bidding with one, two, or three no trump you must have a *balanced hand* and the following point count:

One no-trump: *16 to 18 points.*
Two no-trump: *21 to 23 points.*
Three no-trump: *24 to 26 points.*

When responding to these bids, just add your points to partner's, use your head, and proceed accordingly.

# 4

# The No-Trump Structure

## PART II. Bidding and Responding with Balanced Hands

In the previous chapter we discussed opening bids of one, two, and three no-trump and their responses. But what about balanced hands with a point count different from the requirements to open no-trump? How do you handle a *no-trump type* of hand with 15 or 20 points, for example?

The no-trump structure is the backbone of Standard American bidding, and there's a relatively precise way to handle every *balanced* hand from zero points on up. Once this backbone is mastered, the other bids (bids made with *unbalanced* hands) will fall into place quite easily.

STANDARD AMERICAN BIDDING STRUCTURE
FOR OPENINGS WITH BALANCED HANDS

(4–4–3–2, 4–3–3–3, or 5–3–3–2 PATTERNS)

*With 0 to 12 points*, pass.

Example:
You hold ♠ K J x ♡ A 10 x x ◇ Q J x ♣ J x x.

Pass. Don't open a twelve-point hand unless the points are composed mostly of aces and kings. (With ♠ A x ♡ x x x ◇ A K J 10 ♣ 9 x x x it would be correct to open one diamond.)

*With 13 to 15 points*, (occasionally 12 points) open one of a suit and make a minimum no-trump rebid.

Example:
You hold ♠ A J x ♡ Q x x ◇ A Q x x ♣ J 10 x.

Open one diamond. If partner makes any response which is not forcing (such as one no-trump or two diamonds) you will pass. If he responds one heart or one spade you will rebid one no-trump. If he responds two clubs you will rebid two no-trump. *Your opening bid coupled with your minimum no-trump rebid indicates a balanced hand with 13–15 high card points—or possibly a "good" 12.*

*With 16 to 18 points*, you will of course open one no-trump as discussed in the previous chapter.

*With 19 or 20 points*, (or 18 points with a five-card suit) open one of a suit and jump in no-trump next time.

Example:
You hold ♠ A J x ♡ A J x ◇ A Q J x ♣ Q x x.

Open one diamond. If partner responds one heart or one spade you will jump to two no-trump showing a balanced hand that was slightly too strong for a one no-trump opening but not quite strong enough for an opening two no-trump, i.e., 19 or 20 points. If the response is one no-trump, two clubs or two diamonds, you will jump to three no-trump. Note that you must have a stopper in any unbid suit to jump in no-trump.

A rebid of three no-trump after partner has responded at the one-level, i.e., a double jump, is used to show that the original suit is long and solid and that the hand is strong. The unbid suits must be stopped.

Example:

| SOUTH | NORTH |
|-------|-------|
| 1 ♣   | 1 ♡   |
| 3 NT  |       |

South holds something like:

♠ A x x   ♡ J   ◊ K x   ♣ A K Q x x x x

He expects to take nine tricks once partner has responded, but his hand is not balanced and he may well have a singleton heart. North will normally pass unless he is interested in a slam.

Ocasionally you'll pick up a balanced hand that requires more than two bids to describe.

Example:
You hold   ♠ A J x   ♡ J x   ◊ A K J x   ♣ A Q x x.

This hand has 20 points. You open one diamond and plan to jump to two no-trump over partner's expected response of one heart. But he crosses you up and responds one spade instead. Now you can't bid three no-trump because you haven't got the heart suit stopped. Even if partner's response was a minimum, there should be a good play for game, although you don't know just where at the moment. If you bid two clubs partner may pass. The solution is to bid three clubs, a jump shift, which is forcing to game. Partner's hand might be   ♠ K Q 10 x x   ♡ x x x ◊ Q x x   ♣ x x. The bidding would then proceed:

| YOU | PARTNER |
|-----|---------|
| 1 ◊ | 1 ♠ |
| 3 ♣ | 3 ◊ |
| 3 ♠ | 4 ♠ |

### STANDARD AMERICAN BIDDING STRUCTURE FOR RESPONDING TO AN OPENING BID OF ONE IN A SUIT WHEN YOU HAVE A BALANCED HAND

Now let's discuss the other side of the picture. Suppose your partner opens the bidding with one of a suit and you have a balanced hand. How do you respond?

*With 0 to 5 points*, pass.

Example:
Partner opens the bidding with one diamond. You hold
♠ J x x x  ♡ Q x x  ◇ x x x  ♣ Q x x. Pass. You
don't have enough to respond.

> With 6 to 9 points (*occasionally 10*) without good sup-
> port for partner and with no major suit which can be
> bid at the one level, respond one no-trump.

Example 1.
Partner opens the bidding with one diamond. Next hand
passes. You hold  ♠ K J x  ♡ K x x  ◇ x x x
♣ J 10 x x. Bid one no-trump. This is a very descriptive
bid. Partner will know you have 6 to 9 points and no
major suit.

Example 2.
Partner opens one club. Next hand passes. You hold
♠ x x  ♡ K Q 10 x  ◇ J x x x  ♣ Q x x. Bid one
heart. This is not an exact bid like one no-trump. In
fact, a response of one in a suit could be anywhere from
6 to 18 points and the heart suit could be any length
from four up. It's so important, however, to show a 4-card
major suit you should bid one heart on this hand rather
than one no-trump.

Example 3.
Partner bids one spade. Next hand passes. Again you hold
♠ x x  ♡ K Q 10 x  ◇ J x x x  ♣ Q x x. You can't
bid one heart over one spade, and a bid at the two level
requires about 10 points. Here the correct bid is one no-
trump.

> With 10 to 12 points (*the difficult zone*), it's sometimes
> necessary to manufacture a bid.

Example:
Partner opens one spade. Next hand passes. You hold
♠ J x  ♡ K J x  ◇ A 10 x x  ♣ Q 10 x x. This is a
no-trump type of hand, but it's too strong for a bid of one

no-trump (6 to 9 points) and it's too weak for a response of two no-trump (13 to 15 points). You have about a one-and-a-half no-trump bid. The way to show it is to manufacture a bid of two diamonds. If partner bids two spades you now bid two no-trump. This won't be a jump bid and partner can pass with a minimum. If he holds about 15 points, however, he'll carry on to game, counting on you for about eleven points.

*With 13 to 15 points (and all unbid suits stopped), bid two no-trump.*

Example:
Partner opens one heart. Next hand passes. You hold
♠ A Q x   ♡ J x   ◇ K J x x   ♣ K 10 x x. Bid two no-trump. Partner will know immediately that you have 13 to 15 points, a balanced hand, and stoppers in the other three suits.

*With 16 or 17 points and all unbid suits stopped, bid three no-trump.*

NOTE: Some textbooks still give 16 to 18 points for the jump to three no-trump. Most experts today would make a jump shift with 18 points for fear of missing a slam.

Example:
Partner opens one heart. Next hand passes. You hold
♠ A Q x   ♡ Q 10 x   ◇ A J 10 x   ♣ K 10 x. Bid three no-trump. Partner will know immediately that you have 16 or 17 points, a balanced hand, and all unbid suits stopped.

*With 18 or more points, make a jump shift.*

Example:
Partner opens one spade. Next hand passes. You hold
♠ K x x   ♡ A J   ◇ A K J x x   ♣ K x x. Bid three diamonds. This is a tremendous bid which is not only forcing to game but an invitation to slam.

As a handy reference,

*When it's your turn to open and you hold a balanced hand:*

*With 0 to 12 points*, pass.

*With 12 to 15 points*, bid one of a suit and rebid one no-trump.

*With 16 to 18 points*, bid one no-trump.

*With 19 or 20 points*, bid one of a suit and jump in no-trump on the next round. (Unbid suits must be stopped.)

*With 21 to 23 points*, bid two no-trump.

*With 24 to 26 points*, bid three no-trump.

*When partner opens one of a suit and you hold a balanced hand:*

*With 0 to 5 points*, pass.

*With 6 to 9 points*, without good support for partner and with no major suit that can be bid at the one-level, bid one no-trump. (This bid will sometimes be made with an unbalanced hand, especially if the opening bid is one spade.)

*With 10 to 12 points*, manufacture a bid.

*With 13 to 15 points* and all unbid suits stopped, bid two no-trump.

*With 16 or 17 points* and all unbid suits stopped, bid three no-trump.

*With 18 points and up*, make a jump shift.

Notice that any time opener or responder makes a no-trump bid, his partner should have a pretty good idea of where the hand belongs. All he has to do is to add his points to the precise number shown by the no-trump bidder and bid accordingly.

Example 1.

| SOUTH | NORTH |
|-------|-------|
| 1 ◇ | 1 ♡ |
| 1 NT | ? |

As North you hold ♠ A x x ♡ K J 10 x ◊ Q x x
♣ K J x. You should bid three no-trump. Your 14
points added to the 12 to 15 which partner has announced
bring the partnership total to the 26 points needed for
game.

Example 2.

| SOUTH | NORTH |
|-------|-------|
| 1 ◊ | 2 NT |
| ? | |

As South you hold ♠ A Q x ♡ A Q x ◊ A K J x
♣ 10 9 x. You should bid six no-trump. Your 20 points
added to partner's announced 13 to 15 bring the partnership total to the 33 points required to bid a small slam.

*Because the partner of the no-trump bidder knows so
much about the partnership assets, he becomes temporary
captain of the team. The no-trump bidder himself has
already told his story and should not take drastic action on
his own initiative.*

For example, a bidding sequence like this just doesn't
exist:

| SOUTH | NORTH |
|-------|-------|
| 2 NT | 3 ♡ |
| 6 NT | |

North is the captain of the partnership and South should
have his mouth washed out with soap for that ridiculous
bid of six no-trump. Normally he would be expected to
rebid either three no-trump or four hearts. With an exceptional fit for partner and a maximum count for two
no-trump, South might express his enthusiasm with a cue
bid (below the game level) such as four clubs. *But any
decision to proceed past the game level of four hearts must
come from the captain.*

Occasionally the captain will need to ask the no-trump
bidder a question. For example:

| SOUTH | NORTH |
|-------|-------|
| 1 ♡ | 1 NT |
| 2 NT | |

Here South became captain as soon as North bid one no-trump showing 6 to 9 points. The two no-trump bid asks North if his original response was a maximum or a minimum. North should continue to game if he has 8 or 9 points. He should pass if he holds 6 or 7 points.

Now let's test your knowledge of no-trump bidding with the following quiz:

## QUIZ ON NO-TRUMP BIDDING

In each of the following cases you are the dealer. What do you bid?

| | | | |
|---|---|---|---|
| 1. ♠ A Q x | ♡ A Q x x | ◊ Q x | ♣ K 9 x x |
| 2. ♠ A J x | ♡ K x x | ◊ A J x x | ♣ J 10 x |
| 3. ♠ K J x x | ♡ x x x | ◊ K Q x | ♣ Q J x |
| 4. ♠ A K J x | ♡ Q J 10 | ◊ A J 9 x | ♣ A Q |
| 5. ♠ A Q | ♡ K Q 10 | ◊ A Q x x | ♣ Q x x x |

In each of the following cases partner has opened the bidding with one no-trump. What do you respond?

| | | | |
|---|---|---|---|
| 6. ♠ J x x | ♡ Q x x | ◊ A x x x | ♣ x x x |
| 7. ♠ x x | ♡ 10 9 x x x x | ◊ Q x | ♣ x x x |
| 8. ♠ K Q 10 x x | ♡ A x x | ◊ x x | ♣ J x x |
| 9. ♠ Q x x | ♡ K x | ◊ A Q x x x | ♣ x x x |
| 10. ♠ J x | ♡ A x x | ◊ K 10 x x x | ♣ x x x |
| 11. ♠ A J x | ♡ A K | ◊ Q 9 x x | ♣ K 9 x x |

In each of the following cases partner has opened the bidding with one diamond. What do you respond?

| | | | |
|---|---|---|---|
| 12. ♠ A Q x | ♡ K J x | ◊ x x x | ♣ K J 10 x |
| 13. ♠ A x x | ♡ x x x | ◊ x x | ♣ K J x x x |
| 14. ♠ K J 10 x | ♡ x x | ◊ A x x | ♣ J x x x |
| 15. ♠ K Q x | ♡ A Q x | ◊ A x x | ♣ Q x x x |
| 16. ♠ K x x | ♡ A Q x | ◊ x x x | ♣ Q 10 x x |

What do you bid next in each of the following sequences?

17. SOUTH     NORTH
   1 NT      2 NT
   ?

You hold  ♠ K Q 10  ♡ A x x  ◊ K x x x  ♣ K J x.

18.  SOUTH      NORTH
    1 ◇         1 ♠
    1 NT      2 NT
    ?
You hold   ♠ K x   ♡ A Q x   ◇ K J 10 x   ♣ Q x x x.

19.  SOUTH      NORTH
    1 ◇         1 ♡
    2 NT       ?
You hold   ♠ A J x   ♡ K Q 10 x   ◇ A x   ♣ 10 9 x x.

20.  SOUTH      NORTH
    1 ♣         1 ♡
    2 NT       ?
You hold   ♠ x x x x   ♡ K Q x x   ◇ x x x   ♣ x x.

21.  SOUTH      NORTH
    1 ♣         1 ♡
    1 NT       ?
You hold   ♠ A x x   ♡ K Q x x   ◇ x x x   ♣ J x x.

## Answers to Quiz

1.  Bid one no-trump.
2.  Bid one diamond and plan to rebid one no-trump.
3.  Pass.
4.  Bid two no-trump.
5.  Bid one diamond and plan to jump to two no-trump next round. *Never open one no trump with 19 points.*
6.  Pass.
7.  Bid two hearts.
8.  Bid three spades and let partner choose the final contract of three no-trump or four spades.
9.  Bid three no-trump. Generally you should not bother to show a minor suit when there's no possibility of slam.
10.  Bid two no-trump. Partner will pass with 16 points and bid game with 17 or 18 points.
11.  Bid six no-trump.
12.  Bid two no-trump.

13. Bid one no-trump.
14. Bid one spade.
15. Bid three no-trump.
16. Bid two clubs. If partner rebids two diamonds you can rebid two no-trump.
17. Pass. You have a minimum.
18. Bid three no-trump. You have a maximum for your previous bidding.
19. Bid six no-trump. Your 14 points added to partner's 19 or 20 points bring the partnership total to the 33 points needed for slam.
20. Pass. The partnership total is less than 26 points.
21. Pass. The partnership total is less than 26 points.

RATE YOURSELF AS FOLLOWS:

| | |
|---|---|
| No mistakes ......... | Expert |
| 1 or 2 mistakes ....... | Good |
| 3 to 5 mistakes ....... | Above average |
| 6 to 9 mistakes ....... | Average |
| 10 to 14 mistakes ..... | Better reread "The No-Trump Structure," Parts I and II |
| 15 or more mistakes ... | Have you considered taking up canasta? |

# 5

# The Opening One-Bid

Most players are aware that 13 points make an opening bid, although they may not know why. The reason is this. It has been determined that about 26 points are needed to make a game. No bidding system can be much good if those who use it pass out hands that belong in game. If both partners pass with 13 points each, they may pass out hands worth 26 points and a probable game. It is logical, therefore, that any hand worth 13 or more points should be opened.

## How to Evaluate Unbalanced Hands

While the 4–3–2–1-point count is very satisfactory for no-trump bidding, it is not adequate for bidding unbalanced hands. Several methods have been devised for translating distributional values into point count. The best of these is the following, devised by my husband, Alan Truscott.

*Asset Points for Suit Bidding*
A singleton counts as one asset.
A void counts as two assets.
A long suit (five cards or more) counts as one asset.
An asset is the equivalent of one point.

40

Assets become very significant as the bidding develops, and may boom or slump depending on the degree of fit which is established. An eight-card trump fit is normal, and if you find such a fit the value of your assets does not change. The following table applies:

| | |
|---|---|
| no eight-card fit available | assets slump to zero |
| eight-card fit | assets unchanged in value |
| nine-card fit | assets double |
| ten-card fit | assets triple |
| and so on. | |

(Note: If you are considering opening no-trump at any level, or raising no-trump, a long suit is still an asset but a void or a singleton is not.)

Example:
You hold ♠ A Q 9 4 2 ♡ A 10 7 6 4 ◇ 5 3 ♣ 6.

This hand is worth 13 points (10 points in high cards, plus three assets, one for each of the five-card suits and one for the singleton club. The total, points plus assets, comes to 13, and the hand should be opened with one spade.

### Unguarded Honors

An unguarded honor may be a defect. For example, a singleton king might be no better than a deuce if an opponent led the ace. On the above scale, a singleton king is apparently worth four points, three points as a high card and one singleton asset. This is too much. In the case of a singleton king, queen, or jack count *either* high-card points *or* as an asset. Do not count both. (As we shall see later, when revaluing the hand after uncovering a fit, it may pay to count a singleton king or queen as one asset instead of its high-card value.)

## Judgment

When the value of a hand comes to about 13 points, it is necessary to use a little judgment to decide whether to open the bidding. A very general rule is this: *Always* open a hand worth 14 points. *Usually* open a hand worth 13 points. *Sometimes* open a hand worth 12 points. Base your decision on these *four judgment factors:*

### Judgment Factor 1: "Good Points" versus "Bad Points"

In the 4–3–2–1 point count the ace is slightly undervalued in comparison with the lower honors, and the useful ten is not counted at all. Although queens and jacks pull their weight at no-trump contracts, they are sometimes useless at a suit contract. Consequently, when you bid a suit you should eye with favor any hand well-supplied with aces and tens, and you should discount somewhat any hand where the high-card points consist mostly of queens and jacks (bad points).

### Judgment Factor 2: Quick Tricks

An important factor in estimating the value of a hand is the number of quick tricks it contains. An opening bid promises about two to two and a half tricks. You should rarely pass a hand containing more than two and a half quick tricks, and usually you shouldn't open a hand containing less than two quick tricks.

$$A = 1 \text{ quick trick}$$
$$AK = 2 \text{ quick tricks}$$
$$AQ = 1\tfrac{1}{2} \text{ quick tricks}$$
$$KQ = 1 \text{ quick trick}$$
$$K = \tfrac{1}{2} \text{ quick trick}$$

### Judgment Factor 3: Combination of Honors

A combination of honors is more valuable than the honors would be separately.

Hand A: &spades; A Q J 10 &hearts; x x x &diams; x x x &clubs; x x x
Hand B: &spades; A x x x &hearts; Q x x &diams; J x x &clubs; 10 x x

Hand A is worth more than Hand B.

*Judgment Factor* 4: *The Location of Honors*

Honors are more valuable if they are located in your long suits.

Hand A:  ♠ A K x x x x  ♡ x x x  ◊ x x  ♣ x x

Hand B:  ♠ x x x x x x  ♡ x x x  ◊ x x  ♣ A K

Hand A is worth more than Hand B.

Let's try a few examples using these judgment factors.

Example 1.

♠ K J 8  ♡ Q J 4  ◊ K J 8  ♣ Q 8 3 2

This hand has 13 points but they are "bad" points. An ace-less hand should always be devalued somewhat. Furthermore, it is short of quick tricks. You should pass.

Example 2.

♠ A K 10 9 4 2  ♡ K J 2  ◊ 9 8  ♣ 7 6

In this hand the points are "good" and the honors are well located. Open one spade.

Example 3.

♠ A 9 8  ♡ 6 4 2  ◊ 9 7 5  ♣ A K J 10

Three quick tricks are not to be sneezed at! Open one club.

## Bidding a Major Suit

When you open one heart or one spade, partner will expect you to have five or more cards in the suit and 13 or more points.

Example 1.

♠ K 4  ♡ 10 8 7 5 2  ◊ A K 6  ♣ K 3 2

Open one heart. Do not be put off by the weakness of the suit.

Example 2.
♠ K J 2    ♡ A K Q 10 7 5    ◇ Q J 2    ♣ K

Open one heart. This is a strong hand, but there will be no game if partner cannot respond.


## Bidding a Minor Suit

When you open one club or one diamond you normally hold four or more cards in the suit and 13 or more points.

Example 1.
♠ A Q x x    ♡ K x    ◇ A x x    ♣ J x x x

Open one club.

Example 2.
♠ A x x    ♡ K x    ◇ K Q    ♣ A Q J x x x

Open one club.


## Telling a White Lie

Occasionally you will have an opening hand with no five-card major and no four-card minor. If it does not qualify for a no-trump bid you will have to tell a little white lie.

The whitest lie is to open one club on a good three-card suit.

Example 1:
♠ Q x x x    ♡ Q x x x    ◇ K x    ♣ A K x

It is undesirable to open one heart or one spade here, as partner will expect a five-card suit. It would be a serious distortion of the truth to bid one no-trump or to pass.

The best solution is to open one club. This normally shows four cards, but all partners must be aware that one club is occasionally opened on a three-card suit for purposes of convenience.

Sometimes you may choose to open a strong four-card major.

Example 2.

♠ A x x  ♡ A K Q 9  ◇ x x x  ♣ J x x

Here the choice lies between opening one heart, supposedly showing five or more hearts, and of opening one club to show four or more. Many experts would open one heart here as a lesser evil. They feel that to bid one club on J x x is a double lie: You do not want partner to raise clubs, and you do not want him to lead clubs. On the other hand to open one heart is a rather mild lie. A K Q 9 is virtually the equivalent of many five-card suits.

Other experts would open one club here, preferring at all costs to stick to the five-card major rule. This is a matter of personal preference and judgment. You may open either one heart or one club.

**Never Open a Two-card Suit**

Example:

♠ A x x x  ♡ Q x x x  ◇ A K x  ♣ J x

Open one diamond. It is undesirable to open with a three-card diamond suit, but it would be terrible to open one club with only two cards.

**Choosing the Whiter Lie**

Example 1.

♠ Q 10 x x  ♡ A K x  ◇ K Q x  ♣ J 9 x

Open one no-trump. You are only about half a point short.

Example 2.

♠ 10 x x x  ♡ A x x  ◇ A J x  ♣ A x x

Open one club, not one diamond. When forced to choose between two three-card minors it is better to bid one club than one diamond even if the diamonds are slightly better. Partners are aware that one club is occasionally bid with a three-card suit, but they expect one diamond to show four cards or more.

### Which Suit to Bid First

With a two-suited hand, the general rule is this: With two suits of unequal length, bid the longer one first. With two suits of equal length, bid the higher-ranking one first.

Example 1.
♠ A Q J 9 7   ♡ 5   ◊ A K J 6 4 2   ♣ 4

You should open one diamond, your longest suit. Next round you'll bid spades, and the next round you'll rebid spades. This will show at least five spades (because you bid them twice) and at least six diamonds (the diamond suit must be longer than the spade suit or you wouldn't have bid it first).

Example 2.
♠ K J 6 4 2   ♡ A K Q 8 3   ◊ 6 5   ♣ 4

Open one spade, the higher-ranking of the two five-card suits. Next plan to bid and rebid hearts. This sequence of bids will show at least five cards in both major suits.

The necessity to prepare a convenient rebid for yourself causes exceptions to this general rule.

*Exception* 1.    With an equal number of spades and clubs, bid the club suit first for purposes of economy.

Example:
♠ A Q 6 5 2   ♡ K 8   ◊ 4   ♣ A J 8 6 5

You should open one club. Over partner's expected response of one diamond or one heart, you will bid one spade. The next round you will rebid the spades. Notice that if you open this hand with one spade and partner responds in a red suit, you'll have to go to the three level to show your second suit. By opening with one club, you produce a much more economical auction.

*Exception* 2.    With a minimum hand and two adjacent suits, it's sometimes better to bid the higher-ranking suit first even if the lower-ranking suit is slightly longer. (Adjacent suits, or touching suits, are those which are next to each other in rank: spades and hearts, hearts and diamonds, diamonds and clubs.)

Example:
♠ 6   ♡ A Q 9 8 6   ◇ K Q 6 4 3 2   ♣ 8

You should open one heart. The trouble with opening this hand with one diamond is the rebid situation. If you open one diamond and partner responds one spade and you rebid two hearts, you will have reversed. Whenever you bid two adjacent suits in reverse order you show a very powerful hand. If you open one diamond and rebid two diamonds, you will be telling the truth about your high-card strength but you'll be concealing your valuable five-card major. The best solution is to treat the two suits as though they were of equal length. Open one heart, then bid and rebid diamonds.

## Third-Seat Opening Bids

In third position, the bidding may be opened with about a queen less than in first or second position. The reason is that your partner is a passed hand, and his response therefore will not be forcing. If your opening bid is shaded, you'll simply pass partner's response and play for a part score.

Example:

| SOUTH | WEST | NORTH |
|-------|------|-------|
| Pass  | Pass | ?     |

As North, you hold ♠ Q 4 3   ♡ A K Q 10   ◇ 10 8 5 ♣ 8 7 2. Open one heart. Don't worry about your rebid. You plan to pass whatever partner responds.

### Fourth-Seat Opening Bids

A fourth-seat opening bid promises about the same strength as a bid in first or second position. There is, however, no need to prepare for a rebid, since partner is a passed hand. If you have the spade suit, you'll find it tactically advantageous to open slightly under strength. The reason is that when you contemplate passing out a hand in fourth position, it means that the high cards are fairly evenly distributed around the table. Both sides can probably make a part score in their best suit. The side with spades naturally has a tremendous advantage in any part-score battle.

## QUIZ ON OPENING BIDS

You are the dealer. What do you do with each of the following hands?

1. ♠ K Q 6 3   ♡ Q 4   ◇ Q J 9 5 2   ♣ Q 2
2. ♠ A Q 10 6 5   ♡ A J 9 8   ◇ 4 3 2   ♣ 9
3. ♠ A Q 6 3   ♡ K J 3   ◇ K 6   ♣ K J 10 9
4. ♠ K Q J 6 5   ♡ A 4   ◇ 3   ♣ A 10 9 7 6
5. ♠ A 7   ♡ 4   ◇ A Q 7 5 4   ♣ A K J 5 2

### Answers to Quiz

1. Pass. This 13-point hand should be demoted because the points are "bad," and it doesn't contain two quick tricks.

2. Bid one spade. The hand is worth 13 points (11 points in high cards, one asset for the five-card suit and one for the singleton). With 2½ quick tricks, this is a clear-cut opening bid.
3. Bid one no-trump. Never ignore a good opportunity to make the descriptive bid of one no-trump, showing partner precisely 16 to 18 points in high cards and a balanced hand.
4. Open one club. With equal length in the black suits, bid clubs first.
5. Bid one diamond. With two five-card suits, bid the higher-ranking suit first unless both suits are black.

# 6

# Responses to Opening Bids
## of One in a Suit

When partner opens the bidding he launches your team on a search for game. Let's say he bids one heart. You should assume he has five or more hearts and in the neighborhood of 13 to 20 points. Remember, it takes the equivalent of about 26 points to make a game. If your hand is worth less than 6 points, you should pass. Game is remote.

Example:
Partner opens the bidding with one heart. You hold ♠ Q J 4 2  ♡ J 5  ◇ J 6 2  ♣ 8 6 5 3. You should pass. One heart may not be the ideal spot, but if you act with this hand you will probably get overboard.

If your hand is worth 6 or more points, however, there is a chance of making a game if partner has a maximum.

Example:
Partner deals and bids one heart. You hold  ♠ K Q 7 2. ♡ J 3  ◇ 10 8 7 2  ♣ 8 7 4. You should bid one spade. This hand could produce a game if partner holds something like  ♠ A 6 5 4  ♡ A K Q 9 6 2  ◇ J 7 ♣ 2.

## Raising Partner

The most helpful response is the direct raise, particularly of partner's major-suit bid.

When evaluating your hand for a raise, count your assets and make the necessary adjustments. Remember that they double if you have found a nine-card fit, and so on.

You assume a normal eight-card fit if you have three-card support for an opening major-suit bid, or four-card support for a minor-suit opening. These are minimum requirements for a direct raise: Never raise a major with less than three cards, or a minor with less than four cards.

## The Single Raise (One Heart to Two Hearts)

With the equivalent of 6 to 10 points and at least three trumps, give partner a single raise.

Example: Partner deals and bids one heart. You hold

A. ♠ 6    ♥ A 5 3 2    ♦ Q 10 7 6    ♣ 9 8 6 5
B. ♠ J 3    ♥ K J 5 3 2    ♦ 10 8 7 6    ♣ J 6
C. ♠ 7    ♥ A 9 7    ♦ 10 9 8 4 3    ♣ K 6 3 2
D. ♠ K 9 8 4 2    ♥ K 9 7 5    ♦ 10    ♣ 9 5 2

With each of these hands, your proper response is two hearts. Some players might make the mistake of responding one spade with hand D. This would be poor judgment. The hand is worth only one bid, and your first duty is to support partner's major suit if possible.

The requirements for a raise of a minor suit are about the same as for a major suit. However, it is so important to try to locate the eight-card major-suit fit that you should not raise partner's minor suit if you can bid a major suit yourself.

Example:
Partner deals and bids one diamond. You hold  ♠ K 6 2
♥ 8 7  ♦ K Q 6 5 2  ♣ 10 8 2.  You should respond

two diamonds. However, if you hold ♠ K J 8 2 ♡ 8 7 ◊ K 9 5 4 2 ♣ 10 8 you should bid one spade.

## The Double Raise (One Heart to Three Hearts)

With four trumps and the equivalent of 13 to 16 points, including at least 10 in high cards, give partner a double raise.

Example:
Partner deals and bids one heart. You hold ♠ A 2 ♡ K J 7 3 ◊ K Q 3 ♣ J 7 3 2. You should bid three hearts. Game is assured because the combined point count must be at least 26. Partner cannot pass. (Remember, any jump bid by responder is forcing to game.) If partner has a minimum hand, he will simply rebid four hearts.

The double-raise requirements are about the same in a minor suit as in a major. Again, however, you shouldn't raise the minor immediately if you can bid a good major suit first.

Example:
Partner deals and bids one diamond. You hold ♠ K J 4 ♡ 7 6 ◊ A Q 6 3 2 ♣ K 8 2. You should bid three diamonds. However, if you hold ♠ K J 6 2 ♡ 6 5 ◊ A Q 6 3 2 ♣ K 8 you should bid one spade and plan to jump in diamonds next round.

## The Triple Raise (One Heart to Four Hearts)

This bid describes a hand with especially good trump support (usually five or six trumps and a singleton or a void), but not more than 9 points in high cards. This bid is known as a "shut-out bid" because it serves to keep the enemy out of the auction.

Example:
Partner deals and bids one heart. You hold ♠ 5 ♡ K Q 10 7 2 ◇ Q 10 8 5 3 ♣ 4 2. You should bid four hearts.
Notice that the original three assets have tripled, giving a total value of 16 points—enough to bid game.


## The Temporizing Bid

What about intermediate hands where you have four trumps for partner but only 11 or 12 points?

Example:
Partner deals and bids one spade. You hold ♠ 10 9 5 2 ♡ J 6 ◇ A Q J 8 ♣ K 8 6. This hand is worth 11 points in support of spades. A single raise showing 6 to 10 points would be an underbid, while a double raise showing 13 to 16 points would be an overbid. The proper procedure is to temporize with a bid in your best side suit. Bid two diamonds. If partner rebids two spades, raise him to three spades on the next round.


## The Jump Shift

Normally, a jump shift shows 18 or more points including at least 14 in high cards. With very good trump support, however, it can be made with 17.

Example:
Partner deals and opens one spade. You hold ♠ A 10 5 4 ♡ 8 ◇ K Q J 6 2 ♣ A 7 5. You should bid three diamonds. Next round you will raise spades. This hand is worth 18 points in support of spades—the two assets have doubled on account of the nine-card fit—so it is too strong for a jump to three spades.


## Summary of Raises to Opening Bids of One in a Suit

Partner deals and bids one spade, and you have four spades.

*With 6 to 10 points*, bid two spades.

*With 11 to 12 points*, make a temporizing bid in your best suit, then raise spades next round. Or with especially good trumps and not more than 9 high-card points, make a pre-emptive jump to four spades.

*With 13 to 16 points*, including at least 10 in high cards, bid three spades.

*With 17 points or more*, including at least 14 in high cards, make a jump shift, then support spades on the next round.

## No-Trump Responses to Opening Bids of One in a Suit

Do not count distributional points when bidding no-trump. The no-trump responses to opening bids of one in a suit are discussed in detail in Chapter 4, "The No-Trump Structure." Briefly, they are:

*With 6 to 9 points* (occasionally 10) without good support for partner and with no major suit that can be bid at the one level, bid one no-trump.

*With 10 to 12 points*, make a temporizing bid.

*With 13 to 15 points*, a balanced hand, and all unbid suits stopped, jump to two no-trump.

*With 16 to 17 points*, a balanced hand, and all unbid suits stopped, jump to three no-trump.

*With 18 or more points*, make a jump shift.

## Bidding a New Suit

Responder may bid a new suit at the one level with 6 or more points.

Example:
Partner deals and bids one diamond. Whether you hold ♠ 7 6 4 2 ♡ J 5 ◇ 10 8 6 ♣ A J 8 7 or ♠ A K J 6 2 ♡ 10 ◇ A 6 2 ♣ Q 8 5 2, your proper response is one spade. This simply shows partner that you have at least four spades and a hand worth at least 6 points. For further details he'll have to wait until your next bid.

To bid a new suit at the two level requires a hand worth 10 or more points. Obviously you need more to go to the two level than to respond at the one level.

Example:
Partner deals and opens one heart. You hold ♠ K 8 5 ♡ 8 7 ◇ 9 4 2 ♣ K J 10 8 5. You should bid one no-trump. You don't have enough strength to bid two clubs.

Example:
Partner deals and opens one heart. You hold ♠ A K 6 ♡ 8 7 ◇ 7 4 3 ♣ K J 10 8 5. You should bid two clubs. This time you have sufficient high-card strength to bid at the two level.

## The Jump Shift

A jump shift by responder shows a hand worth about 18 or more points. With a solid suit, or with very good support for partner, it may be made with 17. On the other hand, if you have no strong suit and no support for partner, you need about 19 points.

Example 1.
Partner opens one diamond. You hold ♠ A K Q J 9 7 ♡ — ◇ J 4 2 ♣ A 7 5 2. You should bid two spades. There's no need to search for a trump fit. Your spade suit will be adequate even opposite a void. The jump shift guarantees game and suggests slam possibilities immediately.

The moderate fit in diamonds is an encouraging sign. If the opening bid had been one heart, indicating a misfit, a response of one spade would be adequate.

Example 2.
Partner bids one diamond and you hold ♠ A J 8 6 2 ♡ A Q 6 3 ◇ 8 ♣ A J 9. You should bid one spade. There's so much exploratory work to be done in

55

order to find out where this hand belongs that it's better not to crowd the bidding with a jump shift.

## Which Suit Responder Should Bid First

With two suits of unequal length, the general rule is to bid the longer suit first.

Example:
Partner opens one heart. You hold ♠ A K J 6 ♡ 7 ◊ A Q 7 4 2 ♣ J 8 5. You should bid two diamonds. Next round you will bid spades. Partner will assume you have four spades and longer diamonds.

Occasionally, with a hand not strong enough to go to the two level, it will be necessary to bid a four-card major suit before a longer minor.

Example:
Partner opens one heart. You hold ♠ K J 8 7 ♡ 8 6 ◊ K 9 6 4 2 ♣ 9 7. You should bid one spade. You don't have enough strength to bid two diamonds.

With two five-card suits, or two six-card suits, bid the higher-ranking one first.

Example:
Partner opens one club. You hold ♠ K 9 8 6 3 ♡ A K 9 7 2 ◊ Q 6 ♣ J. You should respond one spade. Next time you will bid hearts.

With two or three four-card suits it is necessary to plan ahead. Always remember that your primary objective is to uncover the eight-card major-suit fit. It's usually best to respond "up the line"; that is, the lower-ranking suit first.

In each of the following examples, partner deals and opens one club.

Example 1.
You hold ♠ K 7 6 2  ♡ Q 6 3 2  ◇ K 8 4 3  ♣ 7.
You should bid one diamond. If partner rebids one heart
or one spade, you will have discovered the eight-card fit
and will give him a single raise next round.

Example 2.
You hold ♠ K J 7 5  ♡ Q 10 8 7  ◇ J 5 4  ♣ J 8.
You should bid one heart. If partner has hearts he'll raise
you, and if he has spades, he can conveniently bid one
spade over one heart, and you will raise him. In either
case the major-suit fit has been uncovered. If, however,
you respond one spade with this hand, it's possible to
miss a four-four heart fit.

### Responding After an Overcall

If your partner opens one of a suit and your right-hand
opponent bids a suit, responses are virtually unchanged
in meaning. If your partner has a strong hand he will
have another chance to bid even if you pass, and any
action by you is called a "free" bid.

A free bid of one no-trump shows a slightly stronger
hand than it would do otherwise.

Example:
As North you hold ♠ K 7 5  ♡ A J 10  ◇ 9 8 7
♣ 10 8 4 2.  The bidding has gone

| SOUTH | WEST | NORTH |
|-------|------|-------|
| 1 ◇ | 1 ♡ | ? |

Bid one no-trump. This will indicate 8-10 points and a
stopper in the opponent's heart suit.

If an opponent makes a jump overcall the situation
changes slightly. Suppose the bidding begins:

| SOUTH | WEST | NORTH |
|-------|------|-------|
| 1 ♡ | 2 ♠ | ? |

Now two no-trump and three hearts would show the equivalent of 10-11 points, not forcing, and slightly less than the same bids made with a jump in the absence of interference.

## QUIZ ON RESPONSES

Partner opens the bidding with one heart. Next hand passes. What do you bid with each of the following hands?

1.  ♠ Q 10 5   ♡ K 6   ◇ A J 4 2   ♣ K J 7 3
2.  ♠ Q J 3 2   ♡ K 5   ◇ 10 9 8 5 3 2   ♣ 2
3.  ♠ 8 6 3   ♡ K 5   ◇ K Q 10 9 5   ♣ 10 8 2
4.  ♠ 7 6   ♡ Q J 9 8 5   ◇ 3   ♣ K J 9 5 4
5.  ♠ A 10 5 4   ♡ A Q 6 3   ◇ 9   ♣ Q 10 8 5
6.  ♠ K J 8 6 4 2   ♡ J 8   ◇ 7 5 2   ♣ 3 2
7.  ♠ K 6 2   ♡ 5 4   ◇ Q 6 4 2   ♣ 9 5 3 2
8.  ♠ 6   ♡ K 8 4   ◇ A K J 10 3 2   ♣ K Q 4
9.  ♠ A J 9 4 3   ♡ 10 8 7 2   ◇ 6   ♣ J 7 2
10. ♠ K J 8   ♡ J 5 4   ◇ A Q 9   ♣ A J 9 2
11. ♠ A Q 3 2   ♡ K 7   ◇ A 10 7 4 2   ♣ 5 4
12. ♠ A 10 8   ♡ 10 8 6 2   ◇ Q 9 5   ♣ A J 6

Partner opens the bidding with one club. Next player passes. What do you do with each of the following hands?

13. ♠ 6 5   ♡ 8 7   ◇ 9 2   ♣ A K Q J 9 7 4
14. ♠ K J 6 2   ♡ 6 4   ◇ 9 8   ♣ K J 7 3 2
15. ♠ K J 7   ♡ 10 8 6   ◇ J 4 3 2   ♣ K 7 4
16. ♠ 7 6 2   ♡ 9   ◇ Q 7 4 2   ♣ K Q 6 4 2
17. ♠ 7 6   ♡ J 7 2   ◇ Q 7 5 4 2   ♣ 10 8 7

**Answers to Quiz**

1.  Two no-trump. This shows 13 to 15 high-card points, a balanced hand, and all unbid suits stopped. It would be poor judgment to respond two clubs or two diamonds here. Never ignore an ideal opportunity

to limit your hand with a precise response of two no-trump.

2. One spade. You don't have enough strength to go to the two level.

3. One no-trump. Again, you don't have enough strength to bid two diamonds.

4. Four hearts. With a ten-card fit your assets have tripled, fully justifying a game bid.

5. Three hearts. Your one asset has doubled, making your total worth 14 points.

6. One spade.

7. Pass. You don't have the 6 to 9 high-card points needed to bid one no-trump.

8. Three diamonds. Either diamonds or hearts will make a good trump suit. Slam is in the wind, and the best way to alert partner is by a jump shift. If he rebids three hearts, simply raise him to four hearts. He'll pass four hearts only if his opening bid was an absolute minimum, lacking controls.

9. Two hearts. This hand is worth one bid and it is far more important to show partner the heart fit than to make the ambiguous response of one spade.

10. Three no-trump.

11. Two diamonds. With adequate strength to bid at the two level, you should bid the longer suit first.

12. Two clubs. Next round, give partner a minimum raise in hearts. This hand is too strong for an immediate single raise to two hearts, and it's too weak for a jump to three hearts. The best solution is to temporize with a bid of two clubs. NOTE: it is not a good idea to temporize in a three-card suit which is higher ranking than partner's suit. In this case, a response of one spade would be dangerous. You might hit partner with four spades, and now you'll never be able to convince him that the hand doesn't belong in spades. It doesn't matter if he raises your clubs, because you can always return to hearts without increasing the level.

13. Three clubs. If partner has a minimum balanced hand, he'll rebid three no-trump. Nine tricks should

be made easily with the opening lead coming up to partner. Your one asset has quadrupled to four, since you have an eleven-card fit.

14. One spade. It's more important to search for the major-suit fit than to support the clubs.

15. One no-trump. A few authorities treat a one no-trump response to a club as a special bid showing 9 to 11 high-card points. Anyone who plays a system that requires a response of one diamond on this hand rather than a straightforward bid of one no-trump is putting himself at a disadvantage. It is more standard among top players to treat a one no-trump response to one club as having the same meaning as a one no-trump response to any other opening bid. Naturally, over one club one would *tend* not to respond one no-trump on a very minimum hand (6 to 7 points), as there are so many cheaper bids available.

16. Two clubs.

17. Pass. It's a losing proposition to keep the bidding open on a hand like this.

# Points, Schmoints! and Rebids by Opener

South deals and opens one spade, holding ♠A 10 8 5 4 3 2 ♡ A Q 4 ◇ — ♣ 10 8 6. The bidding proceeds as follows:

| SOUTH | WEST | NORTH | EAST |
|-------|------|-------|------|
| 1 ♠ | Pass | 2 ♠ | 3 ♡ |
| 3 ♠ | Pass | Pass | Pass |

West leads a heart and North lays down ♠ K 9 7 6 ♡ 7 6 ◇ J 7 5 2 ♣ Q 7 3. South is embarrassed to find that even a half-wit could scarcely fail to take ten tricks with this hand.

North is righteously indignant about the matter, having strained to give his partner a raise on a minimum. If South makes the plaintive excuse, "My hand was only worth 13 points, partner," North is very likely to sneer, *"Points, schmoints!"* This is Expertise. Translated into English it means, "Only an idiot counts points! Why don't you learn to use your head?"

North is only partially correct. Experts *do* count points. But they are not slaves to the point count. *They adjust their evaluation of the hand as the bidding progresses.*

In the example above, South should see that once

North has supported spades he'll probably make seven trump tricks in his hand. Once East has bid hearts, the heart finesse figures to work. And even if North has a minimum raise there will still be a good play for game.

The point count didn't let South down, however. He simply forgot to adjust his assets as the bidding proceeded.

As we have seen earlier, assets double with a nine-card fit and triple with a ten-card fit. In this case South's three assets have tripled because of the known ten-card fit and a bid of four spades is justified. South's total worth is 19, his partner has promised 6 points, and the heart bid on the right has improved the ace-queen combination.

Let's try another example. As South you hold
♠ K J 8 6 5 4 2    ♡ 8    ◇ 9 3    ♣ Q 9 8.

The bidding goes

| NORTH | EAST | SOUTH |
|-------|------|-------|
| 1 NT  | Pass | ?     |

What do you bid?

You picture your partner with a balanced hand with 16-18 high-card points. Most of the time there will be a good play for game, and you should bid four spades directly. Of course you can lay out hands on which the opponents will take the first four tricks, but that is one of the facts of bridge life. You cannot be right all the time.

You would arrive at the correct conclusion by reevaluating your assets. Your partner's one no-trump opening has guaranteed at least two cards in every suit, so you know you have a nine-card fit or better. Your two assets double to four, and your total worth is 10, enough to bid a game combined with your partner's promised 16 points. In fact, much more often than not your partner will have three or four spades for you, and you will have a ten or eleven-card fit.

So if you want to *bid* like an expert, you'll have to learn *to readjust your assets*. And don't forget to mix a strong dash of common-sense into your valuation.

And if you want to *sound* like an expert, you'll have to do it all mentally. Don't mention your assets, and when you talk about points, refer *only to the high-card points*.

## Rebids by Opener

If partner has responded to your opening bid of one in a suit with a direct raise of your suit or with any no-trump bid, you are in command of the situation because you know almost exactly what he has. You'll often be able to place the final contract immediately.

Always keep in mind those three landmarks:

> 26 points make a game
> 33 points make a small slam
> 37 points make a grand slam

Example 1.

| SOUTH | NORTH |
|-------|-------|
| 1 ♠   | 2 ♠   |
| ?     |       |

As South you hold ♠ A Q J 7 4 ♡ K Q 4 2 ◇ 9 7 6 ♣ 3. You must pass. Partner has 6 to 10 points in support of spades. You are assured of a normal eight-card fit, since your partner promises at least three spades. Your two assets are unchanged and your total worth is 14. But the partnership total cannot be more than 24, so you pass. When you know there is no game you should pass at the first convenient opportunity.

Example 2.

| SOUTH | NORTH |
|-------|-------|
| 1 ♠   | 2 ♠   |
| ?     |       |

As South you hold ♠ A Q J 6 4 2 ♡ A 8 5 ◇ 5 ♣ K Q 10. Bid four spades. Partner has 6 to 10 points in support of spades. A nine-card fit is assured, so your two assets have doubled. You have 16 high-card points and your total worth is 20. Combined with the 6 points your partner has promised, you have the values for game and should bid four spades.

Example 3.

| SOUTH | NORTH |
|-------|-------|
| 1 ♠   | 3 ♠   |
| ?     |       |

As South you hold ♠ A Q 9 7 5  ♡ 8  ♢ A K 10 ♣ A 10 8 3. Bid six spades! Partner has shown 13 to 16 points in support of spades. Your hand is now worth 21 points, since your two assets have doubled on the basis of a nine-card fit. This brings the total above the 33 points needed for a small slam. As you have all the suits controlled, you should bid six spades.

Example 4.

| SOUTH | NORTH |
|-------|-------|
| 1 ♠   | 4 ♠   |
| ?     |       |

As South you hold ♠ A Q 10 6 3  ♡ K 10 9 4  ♢ 5 4 ♣ A 5. You should pass. Partner's four-spade bid is primarily pre-emptive. He doesn't have a strong enough hand to bid three spades.

Example 5.

| SOUTH | NORTH |
|-------|-------|
| 1 ♢   | 1 NT  |
| ?     |       |

As South you hold ♠ A 10 4  ♡ 7  ♢ A Q 10 6 4 2 ♣ Q 9 3. Bid two diamonds. Game is out of the question, as partner has only 6 to 9 points. If you had a more balanced hand, you'd pass one no-trump. With a six-card suit and a singleton, however, the hand will play better in diamonds.

## Example 6.

| SOUTH | NORTH |
|-------|-------|
| 1 ♡   | 2 NT  |
| ?     |       |

As South you hold ♠ K 10 5 ♡ A J 9 5 4 ◇ K 9 6 ♣ K 10. Bid three no-trump. Your 14 points added to partner's 13 to 15 points should make game in no-trump an excellent proposition.

## Example 7.

| SOUTH | NORTH |
|-------|-------|
| 1 ♠   | 3 NT  |
| ?     |       |

As South you hold ♠ A Q 8 6 5 ♡ A J 10 6 3 ◇ A 2 ♣ 6. Bid six hearts! Partner has a balanced hand with 16 or 17 points. He's bound to have good support for one of your suits. The partnership values exceed 33 points but don't come up to 37 points. Since you know the hand belongs in a small slam, bid six hearts. This leaves partner the option of returning to six spades if he chooses.

The above examples were all cases where partner's response had limited his hand and you were able to place the contract immediately. Occasionally, however, when partner has limited his hand, you will need to ask him for further details.

## Example 1.

| SOUTH | NORTH |
|-------|-------|
| 1 ♠   | 2 ♠   |
| ?     |       |

As South you hold ♠ A 9 6 4 3 2 ♡ A 6 ◇ Q 4 ♣ K Q 10. Bid three spades. You have a nine-card fit, so your one asset has doubled and your total worth is 17 points. You belong in game if partner has a maximum raise, but you want to stay out of game if partner has a minimum. The solution is to bid three spades. Partner

65

will go on to game if his raise was a maximum, such as ♠ K 8 5 3 ♡ 9 ◇ K 9 8 5 ♣ J 8 4 2. And he'll pass if his raise was a minimum, such as ♠ Q 8 7 5 ♡ 8 7 ◇ K 9 8 5 ♣ J 5 4.

Example 2.

| SOUTH | NORTH |
|-------|-------|
| 1 ♠   | 1 NT  |
| ?     |       |

As South you hold ♠ A Q 10 6 3 ♡ K J 8 ◇ K 10 ♣ A J 9. Bid two no-trump. With 18 high-card points you can expect to make game in no-trump if partner's response was a maximum, but not if he holds a minimum. Partner will carry on to three no-trump with 8 or 9 points, but will pass with 6 or 7 points.

So far we've been discussing hands where partner has limited his holding with a direct raise of your suit or with a no-trump bid. What about the times when partner has responded in a new suit? Suppose the bidding goes

| SOUTH | NORTH |
|-------|-------|
| 1 ♡   | 1 ♠   |

In this case both your hand and partner's are unlimited. You each have only a vague idea of what the other holds. Your rebid may be the key to the whole auction.

## Minimum Rebids (13 to 16 Points)

With a minimum opening bid you must be careful not to push the auction too high with your rebid. Remember, partner may have responded on 6 points, in which case a contract of seven or eight tricks is high enough. A rebid of one no-trump or a single raise of partner's suit, or a rebid of two of your own suit shows you had a minimum opening bid. A rebid of *anything cheaper* than two of your own suit may also be made on a minimum.

Here are some sequences which show a minimum opening bid:

A.  SOUTH    NORTH
    1 ◊      1 ♡
    1 NT

South shows a balanced hand with 13-15 points or the equivalent. Example: ♠ A 5 4   ♡ 10 8 4   ◊ A Q 9 5 ♣ K J 8. If the response was two clubs the rebid would be two no-trump with the same meaning.

B.  SOUTH    NORTH
    1 ◊      1 ♠
    2 ♠

South shows a hand in the minimum range (13 to 16 points), which includes three or four spades. This is one of the few occasions on which an immediate raise can be given with three-card support, since it is a single raise of partner's original major suit. Example: ♠ A 10 6 5 ♡ 8  ◊ A Q J 4  ♣ Q 7 5 2.

C.  SOUTH    NORTH
    1 ◊      1 ♠
    2 ◊

South shows a minimum opening bid with at least a six-card diamond suit. Bidding a suit twice without any hint of support from partner should almost invariably show six or more cards, whether as opener or responder. A five-card suit should only be bid twice in an emergency when no other bid is available. Example: ♠ 7 ♡ A 5 4 ◊ A Q 6 4 3 2  ♣ K 7 5.

Here are some sequences which *may* or *may not* show a minimum opening bid:

D.  SOUTH    NORTH
    1 ♣      1 ♡
    1 ♠

South may have a minimum opening such as ♠ A 10 8 4 ♡ 6 2 ◇ Q 5 4 ♣ A K J 7. Or South may have a strong hand such as ♠ A K 8 5 ♡ 6 2 ◇ K 8 ♣ A K 9 8 2.

E.  SOUTH        NORTH
    1 ◇          1 ♡
    2 ♣

Again South's strength is indeterminate. He could hold either ♠ 2 ♡ 7 6 ◇ A Q 8 6 2 ♣ A J 6 3 2 or ♠ A 4 ♡ 8 ◇ A Q 8 6 2 ♣ A Q 9 8 4.

Notice that in all these examples, the auction wasn't pushed beyond the two level. Particularly look at Example E. If North has a minimum response he can pass two clubs or, if he prefers South's first suit, he can return to diamonds *without going beyond the two level.*

With a weak hand he should give this preference, holding equal length in the minor suits, since he knows that the opener may be longer in diamonds and cannot be longer in clubs.

### Strong Rebids (17 to 19 Points)

Any time the opener pushes the auction to the *three level* with his rebid, he is showing a strong opening (17 to 19 point or the equivalent).

F.  SOUTH        NORTH
    1 ♡          2 ◇
    3 ♣

South must have a strong hand to carry the auction to the three level. For example: ♠ 7 ♡ A Q J 6 5 ◇ K 8 ♣ A Q 7 4 2. If South had this same distribution but a weaker hand, such as ♠ 7 ♡ A Q J 7 4 ◇ 9 8 ♣ A 9 6 4 2, he would have to rebid two hearts over partner's response of two diamonds. This is one of the few occasions on which a rebid of a five-card suit is unavoidable.

**G.** SOUTH     NORTH
    1 ♡        1 ♠
    3 ♡

South shows a strong hand (17 to 19 points) and a long, strong heart suit. Example: ♠ 7 6   ♡ A Q J 9 5 3 ◇ A K 6   ♣ K 2. North may pass with a minimum.

**H.** SOUTH     NORTH
    1 ♡        1 ♠
    3 ♠

South shows a strong hand (17 to 19 points) and four-card support for partner. Example: ♠ Q 9 3 2 ♡ A Q J 8 4 ◇ A 4 ♣ K 6. A normal spade fit is assured, so South can still count his asset for the long heart suit. North may pass with a minimum.

**I.** SOUTH     NORTH
    1 ◇        1 ♠
    2 NT

South shows a balanced hand that was slightly too good to open one no-trump, therefore 19 or 20 points or the equivalent. All unbid suits must be stopped. For example: ♠ 8 7   ♡ A Q 6   ◇ A Q J 9 4   ♣ A J 2. North may pass with a minimum.

**J.** SOUTH     NORTH
    1 ◇        1 ♠
    2 ♡

South's two-heart bid here is called a "reverse." Notice that South has bid two suits in reverse order (the lower-ranking suit before the higher-ranking one) so that if North simply wants to return to South's first suit, diamonds, he is forced to bid at the three level. Because South may be forcing the auction to the *three level*, he is showing a strong hand (17 to 19 points). Because he bid the diamonds first, North can assume he has more dia-

monds than hearts. Example: ♠ A 4  ♡ A K 6 5
♢ A Q 10 8 7  ♣ 8 7. Notice that the sequence

| SOUTH | NORTH |
|-------|-------|
| 1 ♢ | 1 ♡ |
| 1 ♠ | |

is not a "reverse" although technically South has bid two
suits in reverse order. The term "reverse" is applied only
to a *strength-showing reversal of suits, which may force
partner to give a preference at the three level.*

## Gigantic Rebids (20 Points or More)

Any time the opener has a hand worth 20 or more
points he knows his team has a game even if partner's
response was a minimum. In the sequence

| SOUTH | NORTH |
|-------|-------|
| 1 ♡ | 1 ♠ |
| ? | |

North can be presumed to hold at least 6 points. Therefore, if South has 20 points, the partnership must have at
least 26 points and belongs in game. The only forcing
bid which South can make at this point is a jump shift.
Thus with a gigantic hand (20 points or more) South has
to either jump to game himself or make a jump shift to
ensure that North won't pass below game.

K.
| SOUTH | NORTH |
|-------|-------|
| 1 ♡ | 1 ♠ |
| 4 ♠ | |

South shows a powerful hand with good four-card spade
support, such as ♠ A J 8 5  ♡ A Q J 4 2  ♢ A 7
♣ K 6. He expects to take ten tricks even if North has
a minimum.

L.
| SOUTH | NORTH |
|-------|-------|
| 1 ♡ | 1 ♠ |
| 4 ♡ | |

South shows a powerful hand with a long, self-supporting heart suit. Example: ♠ A 5 ♡ K Q J 10 6 5 4 ◇ K Q 7 ♣ 9. He wants to be in game even if North's response was a minimum.

M. SOUTH     NORTH
    1 ◇        1 ♡
    2 ♠

South shows a powerful hand with 20 or more points. For example, South may hold ♠ A K Q 8 ♡ K J 4 ◇ A Q 10 9 6 ♣ 4. Once North has bid one heart, South knows the hand belongs in game, but he's not certain just where. He doesn't dare jump to four hearts because North may have bid on a four-card suit. And he doesn't dare rebid only one spade for fear that North may pass. The solution is to bid two spades and postpone the final decision until he hears partner's next bid.


# QUIZ ON REBIDS

In each of the following hands you are South. What is your next bid?

1. SOUTH     NORTH
    1 ♠        1 NT
You hold ♠ A J 8 4 2 ♡ K Q ◇ Q 4 3 ♣ Q 8 6.

2. SOUTH     NORTH
    1 ♠        1 NT
You hold ♠ A J 10 6 3 ♡ Q 3 2 ◇ A Q 5 4 ♣ 9.

3. SOUTH     NORTH
    1 ♡        1 ♠
You hold ♠ A J 7 ♡ A Q 9 5 4 ◇ 6 5 ♣ K 6 5.

4. SOUTH    WEST    NORTH    EAST
    1 ◇     Pass     1 ♡      1 ♠
You hold ♠ A 4 3 ♡ 9 2 ◇ A Q J 2 ♣ Q 4 3 2.

5.   SOUTH        NORTH
      1 ♦          1 ♥
You hold  ♠ A Q 3  ♥ 8 7  ♦ A Q J 8 2  ♣ K Q 5.


6.   SOUTH        NORTH
      1 ♠          2 ♥
You hold  ♠ A Q 10 6 3  ♥ K 8 4  ♦ A 3 2  ♣ 8 7.


7.   SOUTH        NORTH
      1 ♦          1 ♥
You hold  ♠ A 4 3  ♥ 8  ♦ A K J 6 4  ♣ A Q 5 4.


8.   SOUTH        NORTH
      1 ♣          1 ♠
You hold  ♠ 8 6  ♥ A J 7 6  ♦ Q 8 5  ♣ A Q J 8.


9.   SOUTH        NORTH
      1 ♦          1 ♥
You hold  ♠ A 10 6 2  ♥ Q 4  ♦ A Q J 6 5  ♣ 5 4.


10.  SOUTH        NORTH
      1 ♣          1 ♠
You hold  ♠ A J 8 6  ♥ Q 2  ♦ K 6  ♣ A Q J 7 5.


11.  SOUTH        NORTH
      1 ♣          1 ♠
You hold  ♠ A J 4 3  ♥ Q 2  ♦ A 6  ♣ A K J 6 3.


12.  SOUTH        NORTH
      1 ♦          1 ♠
You hold  ♠ A 4  ♥ A K 9 6  ♦ A Q J 8 7  ♣ 8 7.


13.  SOUTH        NORTH
      1 ♥          1 ♠
You hold  ♠ A J 8  ♥ A Q J 9 6  ♦ A K 7  ♣ J 5.

## Answers to Quiz

1. Pass. There's not much hope of game, since partner has only 6 to 9 points. Your hand is satisfactory for no-trump. Remember that rebidding the spades would show six or more cards.

2. Two diamonds. Game is out of the question. However, it is generally unwise to leave partner in one no-trump when you have a singleton. Two diamonds is the most flexible rebid. Partner may pass if he prefers diamonds to spades, and he'll take you back to spades with equal length in both your suits.

3. Two spades. The immediate raise of partner's suit, if it is a major, can be made with three-card support.

4. Pass. When an opponent relieves you of the obligation to bid, the way to show that your opening was a minimum is to pass.

5. Two no-trump. Don't ignore an opportunity to describe your hand with a precise bid, such as the rebid of two no-trump show stoppers in both unbid suits and a balanced hand too strong for an opening one no-trump—19 or 20 points or the equivalent.

6. Three hearts. A minimum rebid. A raise of partner's first suit is always acceptable with three-card support if it is a major. This particular response, two hearts to one spade, guarantees at least a five-card suit.

7. Two clubs. You have a good hand, but it did not improve when partner bid one heart. Your partner has bid your singleton so the indications are that the hand is a misfit. Your two assets are now worthless and you can only count your 18 high-card points. If partner had responded one spade, you would have the right to assume there was a game somewhere, and a jump shift to three clubs would be called for. Over the one-heart response, a rebid of two clubs is sufficient.

8. One no-trump. It's a shame to conceal the heart suit, but a two-heart bid at this point would be a reverse. Any time you bid two suits in such a way that responder may have to go to the *three level* to take

73

you back to your first suit you show a very strong hand. The proper rebid with this minimum hand is one no-trump, showing a balanced hand and 12 to 15 high-card points.

9. One spade. A new suit at the one level may be bid with a minimum.

10. Three spades. This tells partner you have four spades and a strong hand. He'll pass only if his response was a bare minimum.

11. Four spades. Even if partner has a bare minimum, you want to be in game with this hand.

12. Two hearts. You have ample values for your reverse. Notice that the sequence one diamond, one spade, two hearts is roughly the equivalent of the sequence one diamond, one spade, three diamonds. If your heart six were the diamond six in this example, you'd rebid three diamonds.

13. Three diamonds. A jump shift is often made when opener knows there is a game but doesn't know where. This hand belongs in four spades if North has a five-card suit and in four hearts if North has three hearts. If there is no eight-card major fit, the hand will play in three no-trump if partner has club strength. It would be foolish for South to take a chance and bid four spades, or four hearts, or three no-trump, because he may not choose the right one. By making a jump shift, he can force North to make another bid, which will probably clear up the whole problem. Occasionally a jump shift has to be made on a three-card suit.

# 8

# Opening Bids of More Than One

## Strong Opening Two-Bids

Occasionally you will pick up a hand so strong that you'll expect to make game with almost no help from partner. For example, ♠ A K J 9 6   ♡ A Q J 10 5 ◊ 5 ♣ A K. This hand should take ten tricks in either spades or hearts (depending on which suit partner has more of) even opposite a Yarborough. Yet if you open one spade, partner will pass with less than six points and you'll wind up playing this beauty at one spade. The solution is to open with a bid of two spades.

The opening bid of two of a suit shows a very powerful hand *including at least four quick tricks* (usually more) and an expectation of game with almost no help from partner. It is forcing on both players all the way to game.

If partner has less than about a trick and a half, he makes the negative and artificial response of two no-trump. Thereafter the bidding is natural.

Example:

                    NORTH
              ♠ 4 3
              ♡ 6 4 3
              ◇ Q 6 3 2
              ♣ Q 7 5 2

                    SOUTH
              ♠ A K J 9 6
              ♡ A Q J 10 5
              ◇ 5
              ♣ A K

The bidding:

        SOUTH        NORTH
         2 ♠          2 NT
         3 ♡          3 NT
         4 ♡          Pass

Any response other than two no-trump is positive. That is, it shows about a trick and a half or better. A positive response opposite an opening bid of two in a suit is usually sufficient to produce a slam, provided a trump fit can be found and the necessary controls are present.

Example:

                    NORTH
              ♠ Q 4 2
              ♡ Q 7 5 3
              ◇ A 10 7 6
              ♣ K 6

                    SOUTH
              ♠ A K J 8 7 5
              ♡ —
              ◇ K 5
              ♣ A Q J 10 5

The bidding:

        SOUTH        NORTH
         2 ♠          3 ♠
         4 ♣          4 ◇
         4 ♡          5 ♣
         7 ♠

South opens two spades because he expects to make game with practically no help from partner.

North's three-spade response indicates trump support as well as a trick and a half or better.

Now that trump has been agreed upon, South sets about discovering if the necessary controls are present. Notice that he doesn't use Blackwood because he's not interested in the number of aces and kings in partner's hand. He's interested in a *specific* ace and a *specific* king. So he gives his partner the chance to show *specific* controls. Once he learns that North has both key cards, South confidently bids the grand slam.

### Pre-emptive Bidding

Opening bids of three or four of a major suit and three, four, or five of a minor are known as pre-emptive bids.

Suppose you hold ♠ K Q J 9 8 6 5 4 ♡ 2 ◇ 10 8 ♣ 3 2. This is an ideal pre-empt because the hand will take a large number of tricks if spades are trumps, but it may take no tricks at all if spades are not trumps. Obviously you should be willing to go to some lengths to ensure that spades are trump.

A pre-emptive bid is a sort of *advance sacrifice*. In effect you are offering to pay the opponents to let you play the hand in spades. The mechanics of scoring are such that about 500 points is the right price to offer.

Example:

```
                    YOUR PARTNER
                    ♠ 7 3
                    ♡ K 6 5 4
                    ◇ J 5
                    ♣ J 10 7 5 4

    WEST                            EAST
    ♠ A 2                           ♠ 10
    ♡ A Q 9                         ♡ J 10 8 7 3
    ◇ Q 9 4 3 2                     ◇ A K 7 6
    ♣ K Q 8                         ♣ A 7 6

                    YOU
                    ♠ K Q J 9 8 6 5 4
                    ♡ 2
                    ◇ 10 8
                    ♣ 3 2
```

East-West are vulnerable and you deal. As you expect to win seven tricks if spades are trumps, you can afford to bid four spades. If the opponents let you play four spades doubled, you will be down 500 points. Obviously, this is a tremendous bargain, because East-West belong in six diamonds, which is worth 1570 points (at rubber bridge). Six hearts would also succeed.

Naturally East-West suspect they are being swindled, but it's very hard for them to start looking for their diamond fit at the five level.

The chief advantage of the pre-emptive bid is that it makes life miserable for the opponents. The higher the pre-empt the tougher it is for them to get together. You'll often see an inexperienced player open only three spades with the South hand shown above. He has a parsimonious horror of going down 500 points and hopes to get away for 300 instead. The penny pincher soon regrets his niggardliness, however, because over an opening bid of three spades East-West have a much better chance of finding their slam. Even if they stop at five diamonds or four hearts they will score 820 or 880. They can't have good enough spades to be tempted to settle for three spades doubled. The bait isn't attractive enough.

What do you do when partner opens with a pre-empt and you hold a good hand? Simply add your tricks to those shown by partner and act accordingly. If partner opens three hearts (not vulnerable), you know he is overboard by three tricks or 500 points if doubled. In other words, he expects to win six tricks. If you hold ♠ A 5 4 ♡ 6 2 ◇ A K 6 3 2 ♣ A 7 6 you can expect to contribute four tricks, so you should raise to four hearts. Partner probably holds something like ♠ 8 7 ♡ K Q J 8 7 4 3 ◇ 5 ♣ 9 3 2.

In all cases the partner of the pre-emptive bidder is the captain and is in complete charge of the rest of the auction. His is the responsibility to determine how high to bid or whether to sacrifice. The pre-emptive bidder has already told his whole story and should hold his peace forever after unless partner forces him to bid. A new suit by responder below game level is forcing. Example:

| SOUTH | WEST | NORTH | EAST |
|-------|------|-------|------|
| 3 ♡   | Pass | 3 ♠   | Pass |
| ?     |      |       |      |

South must bid again.

Here's an example of pre-emptive bidding from an all expert game; East-West are vulnerable and South deals:

                    NORTH
                 ♠ 6 4 3
                 ♡ J 10 9 3
                 ◇ 5
                 ♣ K 7 5 4 3

        WEST                        EAST
     ♠ A Q 9 8 7              ♠ K J 10 2
     ♡ K 6 4                  ♡ A Q 8 7 5
     ◇ K J 10 3               ◇ A Q 9 8
     ♣ Q                      ♣ —

                    SOUTH
                 ♠ 5
                 ♡ 2
                 ◇ 7 6 4 2
                 ♣ A J 10 9 8 6 2

The bidding:

| SOUTH | WEST | NORTH | EAST |
|-------|------|-------|------|
| 3 ♣ | Double | 7 ♣ | 7 ♡ |
| Pass | Pass | Pass | |

South started proceedings with a bid of three clubs, and West doubled. (A double of an opening three-bid is for take-out.) North could see that the opponents probably had a grand slam. Almost any nonvulnerable sacrifice is peanuts compared with a vulnerable grand slam, so he jumped promptly to seven clubs.

East found himself on the horns of dilemma. If North had frugally bid only six clubs, East would have had some room left to maneuver. He then could have bid seven clubs himself and forced West to pick a suit. West would have bid seven spades, which he would have made for a score of 2410 points. But over seven clubs, East had a very tough decision to make. He guessed wrong when he bid seven hearts.

North naturally passed. He didn't propose to give the enemy a chance to change its mind.

East-West could have made seven diamonds or seven

spades. But at seven hearts North had to win a trump trick. So, thanks to excellent pre-emptive bidding. North-South came out with plus 100 points instead of minus 2410 points!

## QUIZ ON STRONG OPENING TWO-BIDS

As dealer you hold the following hands. What do you bid?

1. ♠ K Q 10 9 7 6 4 3    ♡ Q J 10 9    ◇ A    ♣ —
2. ♠ A Q 10 9 6    ♡ A K 10 9 6 5    ◇ A    ♣ 5
3. ♠ A K 9 3    ♡ A Q 7 6    ◇ 4    ♣ A K 8 6

Partner opens the bidding with two hearts. Next hand passes. What do you respond with each of the following hands?

4. ♠ 10 8 4 2    ♡ 7 6    ◇ 8 6 4 2    ♣ 5 3 2
5. ♠ Q J 8 6 4 3    ♡ 7 5    ◇ Q J 8    ♣ J 6
6. ♠ Q 9 6 5    ♡ 6 4    ◇ K 10 8 4    ♣ A 10 9
7. ♠ 7 5    ♡ K 7 5 2    ◇ A J 6    ♣ J 6 4 3
8. ♠ A 4    ♡ 8 5    ◇ K Q J 9 6 4    ♣ 7 3 2

**Answers to Quiz**

1. One spade. Even though you expect to take ten tricks if spades are trumps, this hand is not an opening two-bid. You do not have four quick tricks. Don't worry about being passed out at the one level. As you have only 12 points, the other three hands have 28 points and someone is bound to keep the bidding open. The trouble with opening this hand with two spades is that partner may well have a very big hand and push you too high.
2. Two hearts. You expect to make game with almost no help from partner. ⸱
3. One club. This is a very awkward hand to bid. It's true that by opening one club you'll *occasionally* miss a game when partner has a major-suit fit with you

and too few points to keep a one-bid alive. However, if you open with a two-bid you'll often have difficulty reaching the proper contract. You have three possible trump suits in mind. If partner doesn't have a fit for any of them, the best spot may be three no-trump. Unfortunately, after an opening two-bid, you may be well past the game level by the time you've investigated all the possibilities. The best solution is to open one club, planning to rebid two hearts over partner's expected response of one diamond.

4. Two no-trump. Do not consider passing. An opening two-bid in a suit is forcing to game. The proper response with no points up to about a trick and a half is two no-trump.

5. Two no-trump. It's unwise to make a positive response with no aces or kings in your hand. You can bid spades next round.

6. Three no-trump. This shows about 8 to 10 points. Remember that two no-trump denies holding a trick and a half.

7. Three hearts. This shows heart support and about a trick and a half or more.

8. Three diamonds. You have the values for a positive response, so you bid naturally.


## QUIZ ON PRE-EMPTIVE BIDDING

With each of the following hands you are the dealer and neither side is vulnerable. What do you bid?

1. ♠ 7  ♡ 8  ◇ K Q 10 8 7 5 4 3 2  ♣ 9 2
2. ♠ Q 4 3  ♡ J 9 7 5 4 3 2  ◇ J 7  ♣ 2
3. ♠ K Q J 10 5 4  ♡ 4  ◇ J 6  ♣ A 10 9 6
4. ♠ J 10 9 8 6 4 3  ♡ Q 8 4 2  ◇ A 2  ♣ —
5. ♠ Q J 10 8 6 5 3  ♡ 8 7  ◇ —  ♣ J 10 8 2

With each of the following hands you are North, not vulnerable, against vulnerable opponents. South deals and bids three spades. West passes. What do you bid?

6. ♠ 8 7   ♡ A 9 7 4 3   ◇ K 6 2   ♣ A 10 4
7. ♠ A 9 7 4   ♡ 8 2   ◇ K 9 8 3   ♣ Q 6 4

With each of the following hands you are North, not vulnerable, against vulnerable opponents. South deals and bids three spades. West doubles. What do you bid?

8. ♠ A 9 8 6 4 2   ♡ 7   ◇ 9 3   ♣ J 10 9 6
9. ♠ 7   ♡ K J 9 8   ◇ A Q J 3   ♣ K Q 10 6
10. You are South, not vulnerable, against vulnerable opponents. The bidding proceeds

| SOUTH | WEST | NORTH | EAST |
|-------|------|-------|------|
| 3 ♠ | 4 ♠ | 5 ♠ | 7 ♡ |

You hold ♠ K Q 10 9 7 5 4   ♡ —   ◇ J 5 3   ♣ 9 8 2. What do you bid?

## Answers to Quiz

1. Five diamonds. This is an ideal hand for a pre-empt. You expect to take eight tricks if diamonds are trumps and probably none if they aren't.
2. Pass. Your suit is too anemic. A three-heart bid on this hand could cost 900 to 1100 points, which is too steep a price.
3. Bid one spade. Do not pre-empt when you have an opening one-bid. An opening three-bid always shows a hand that is not good enough for an opening one-bid.
4. Pass. You have too many possible defensive tricks on the side. Furthermore it's unwise to open with a three-bid when you have four cards in the other major. You may be pre-empting your own side out of a good heart contract.
5. Three spades. At spades you should win five trump tricks and one club.
6. Pass. You have just enough strength to give partner a chance to make three spades. Remember, he expected to be set three tricks if you were broke.

83

7. Four spades. You don't expect to make it, but East-West must be able to make at least a game. East has a tremendous hand, and it's going to be much harder for him to start guessing over four spades than over three spades.

8. Six spades. You are lucky that your suit is spades, since the enemy cannot possibly outbid you. If worse comes to worst, you are prepared to sacrifice at seven spades. But there's no harm here in trying to buy the hand for six spades doubled. If East-West bid seven of a red suit, you will take out insurance by bidding seven spades. And if they should stumble into seven clubs, you'll innocently pass, trying desperately not to look like the cat that swallowed the canary.

9. Redouble. West has gotten a little too fresh this time. When the hand is over he should be about 1100 points poorer if not any wiser.

10. Pass. It's true that seven spades will be a cheap sacrifice if East-West can make their slam. But partner knows that, too. Furthermore, partner knows what you have in your hand, and you don't know what he has. He's the captain and you must leave the decision to him. Maybe he has a sure trick against seven hearts.

# 9

# Competitive Bidding

About half the time you must expect an opponent to open the bidding. Of course this doesn't mean that you should automatically retire from the field of battle. It does mean, however, that the wrong action by you can be very dangerous. If you interfere and get caught, it can easily cost you 700 to 1100 points.

The most noticeable difference between the bidding of an expert and that of the average player is the expert's agility in competitive situations. He is able to hop in and out of the auction in a high percentage of hands *and rarely gets caught*. The average player is much less aggressive in competitive bidding, and when he does butt in *he frequently gets caught*.

The reason is that the expert has more defensive weapons at his command and knows when and how to use them.

## The Overcall

The best-known defensive weapon is the simple overcall.

In deciding whether or not to overcall you should not think in terms of point count. The important consideration is the quality of your suit. Remember, when you overcall, your left-hand opponent (L.H.O.) may be in an excellent position to inflict a penalty double because he knows his partner has an opening bid.

Suppose you're South and hold ♠ Q J 7 ♡ K J 8 7 4 ◇ A 4 ♣ Q 6 3.

The bidding goes    EAST      SOUTH
                    1 ♠        ?

You should pass! Don't bid two hearts. If West has good hearts and is short in spades, he'll be delighted to double and you may wind up taking only three or four tricks. If you are not vulnerable, this could cost you up to 900 points; if you are vulnerable the carnage could be as much as 1400 points. Partner is not going to be impressed by the excuse that you held 13 points!

To overcall with two hearts, you should hold a hand like ♠ 4 3 ♡ A Q J 10 8 7 ◇ A J 9 ♣ 9 2. Notice that even if everything goes wrong you can't get hurt seriously with this holding because of the good texture of your trump suit. In other words, an overcall at the two level resembles an opening bid with *a long, solid trump suit*.

At the one level, the requirements aren't quite so strict because it's much more difficult to punish a one-level contract. If R.H.O. opens one diamond, it's correct to overcall with one heart holding any of the following:

♠ 10 7   ♡ A J 10 9 3   ◇ 5 4   ♣ K J 10 6
♠ 8   ♡ K Q 10 9 5 4   ◇ 8 7 5   ♣ A 10 2
♠ 7 4   ♡ A K Q 10 6   ◇ J 3   ♣ A Q 7 4

When you are making an overcall, it is essential to keep the vulnerability in mind. With favorable vulnerability (when you are nonvulnerable versus vulnerable opponents), overcalls are apt to be light because the prospects of a sacrifice are good. With unfavorable vulnerability (when you are vulnerable versus nonvulnerable opponents) overcalls should be sound. Prospects of a sacrifice are negligible and the danger involved is great.

If your side doesn't buy the contract, your overcall will

have an influence on the defense, particularly the opening lead. For this reason, avoid overcalling in a suit you don't care to see led.

## The Jump Overcall—Weak or Strong?

Suppose the bidding goes

| EAST | SOUTH |
|------|-------|
| 1 ◇ | 2 ♡ |

What does South's two-heart bid mean? Today there are two schools of thought on the best meaning for the jump overcall:

(1) The more conservative school treats it as a strong bid. If South were playing strong jump overcalls, he'd hold something like

Hand A:  ♠ 7  ♡ A K Q 10 8 6  ◇ 6 5 4  ♣ A Q 9

The requirements are a very sound opening bid with a strong, self-sufficient suit.

(2) The newer school treats South's two-heart bid as weak. Playing weak jump overcalls, often referred to as pre-emptive jump overcalls, South would hold something like

Hand B:  ♠ 8  ♡ Q J 10 8 7 5  ◇ 6 4  ♣ K J 9 4

The requirements are about the same as for an opening weak two-bid.

A few years ago the strong jump overcall was considered "standard." Today, both interpretations are so widely used that neither one can claim to be standard. When you sit down with a stranger you simply have to agree ahead of time whether you are going to play strong or weak jump overcalls.

## Which Method Is Better?

Those experts who advocate weak jump overcalls stress the pre-emptive value of the bid. They also point out that Hand B occurs more frequently than Hand A, and that there are other ways to bid Hand A when it does come up. Those experts who prefer strong jump overcalls point out that the "other" ways to bid Hand A are not ideal. They follow the general principle that it's more important to be sure of arriving at the best contract when you have the cards than it is to attempt to confuse the enemy when you don't have the cards. Finally, the conservatives point in amused horror at the occasional disasters caused by the use (or generally the misuse) of the weak jump overcall.

There's merit in both arguments. However, I've never felt strongly that one method was better than the other. I play weak jump overcalls about half the time, and strong jump overcalls the other half depending on my partner at the moment. I've observed over the years that expert players will do about equally well using either method. Players who are not experts, however, do *worse* with weak jump overcalls due to the disaster-prone nature of the bid.

## The Double-Jump Overcall

Suppose the bidding goes

| SOUTH | WEST |
|-------|------|
| 1 ♣ | 3 ♠ |

West's bid of three spades shows a long (usually seven-card) spade suit and very little defensive strength; for example, ♠ A Q J 9 6 4 2  ♡ 7 4 2  ◇ 5  ♣ 10 8. In other words it looks just like an opening three-spade bid and serves the same pre-emptive purpose. Let's look at a complete hand:

```
                    NORTH
                 ♠ K 10
                 ♡ K J 9 6
                 ◇ A Q 6 4
                 ♣ J 6 5

    WEST                          EAST
 ♠ A Q J 9 6 4 2              ♠ 8 7 5
 ♡ 7 4 2                      ♡ Q 5
 ◇ 5                          ◇ J 10 9 7 2
 ♣ 10 8                       ♣ A 3 2

                    SOUTH
                 ♠ 3
                 ♡ A 10 8 3
                 ◇ K 8 3
                 ♣ K Q 9 7 4
```

South deals and bids one club.

North and South can make a game in hearts, and if
left to themselves will surely bid it. But if West makes a
pre-emptive overcall of three spades, North and South are
going to have a very tough time finding that heart fit.
They may even wind up at three no-trump, which can't be
made.

**The Triple-Jump Overcall**

Suppose the bidding goes

```
        EAST      SOUTH
        1 ♣       4 ♠
```

Here, South's hand may resemble an opening four-spade
bid, such as  ♠ K Q J 10 7 5 4 2  ♡ 7  ◇ 8  ♣ Q 4 2.
South may also have a stronger hand, such as
♠ A K Q 10 6 4 2  ♡ K Q 10  ◇ 7  ♣ 8 5. Notice
that the last hand is too strong for an *opening* four-spade
bid, since partner could easily pass holding sufficient
values for a slam. Once East has opened the bidding,

however, South gives up hope for a slam and makes a tactical overcall of four spades.

The average player overlooks many opportunities to rob the opponents of their bidding space by using double- and triple-jump overcalls.


### The One No-Trump Overcall

An immediate overcall of one no-trump shows an ordinary 16-to-18-point opening no-trump bid with at least one stopper in the opponent's suit. If the bidding goes

|   EAST   |   SOUTH   |
|----------|-----------|
|   1 ♡    |   1 NT    |

then South holds a hand something like ♠ K 10 3 ♡ A J 7 ◇ K J 10 2 ♣ K Q 8.


### The Take-out Double

Suppose the bidding goes

|   EAST   |   SOUTH   |
|----------|-----------|
|   1 ◇    |   Double  |

It would be impractical to use this double for penalties because the hand on which South can expect to punish a one-level bid in this situation almost never arises. Rather than keep the bid idle, bridge players have been using the double of an opening suit bid for the last fifty years (even before the introduction of contract bridge) as a take-out double.

South's double of East's opening bid of one diamond conveys the following message: "I have an opening bid, too, and am probably short in diamonds." In this sequence, South might hold something like ♠ A Q 6 5 ♡ K Q 7 2 ◇ 8 ♣ K J 9 2. With ideal distribution (4-4-4-1 and the singleton in opponent's suit), you may shade the requirements for the take-out double to slightly less than an opening bid. Holding ♠ A 9 5 4 ♡ A J 9 7 ◊ 8 ♣ J 10 8 7 you don't quite have an opening bid, but you do have a double of an opening one-diamond bid. The reason is that you have an excellent chance of finding a fit in any one of three suits. But in general the take-out double promises an opening bid, and there is no maximum.

Naturally you can't always have perfect distribution. However, you may compensate for imperfect distribution with additional strength. With any of the following hands you should double an opening bid of one diamond:

Hand A: ♠ K Q 7 6 ♡ A J 3 2 ◊ 8 ♣ 10 9 7 2
Hand B: ♠ A Q 5 4 ♡ K J 9 ◊ 6 5 ♣ Q 10 8 7
Hand C: ♠ A K 3 2 ♡ A Q J 9 3 ◊ 5 4 ♣ J 2
Hand D: ♠ A 4 3 ♡ K 9 8 ◊ 4 3 2 ♣ A K Q 5

Look at Hand C. The distribution is far from ideal, but it's correct to double. If partner responds in hearts or spades you are delighted, and if he bids two clubs, you have sufficient strength to bid two hearts. It would be poor judgment simply to overcall one heart on this hand, because you can easily miss a good spade fit.

### Responding to a Take-out Double

Example 1.
As South you hold ♠ K 9 5 4 ♡ 4 2 ◊ K J 5 4 ♣ 9 6 5. The bidding goes

| WEST | NORTH | EAST | SOUTH |
|------|-------|------|-------|
| 1 ♣ | Double | Pass | ? |

What do you bid? The answer is one spade. With two suits of equal length, prefer the major.

Example 2.
As South you hold ♠ 9 6 5 4 ♡ 6 5 ◊ 8 7 5 3 2 ◊ 9 2. The bidding goes

| WEST | NORTH | EAST | SOUTH |
|------|-------|------|-------|
| 1 ◊ | Double | Pass | ? |

What do you bid? The answer is one spade. This isn't a hand to be proud of, but partner has asked you to bid your longest suit outside of diamonds and you have no choice. The responsibility is his, not yours.

Example 3.
You are South and hold ♠ Q 7 5 4  ♡ J 8 7  ◊ 9 2
♣ 8 7 3 2.   The bidding goes

| WEST | NORTH | EAST | SOUTH |
|------|-------|------|-------|
| 1 ◊ | Double | 1 ♡ | ? |

What do you bid? The answer is pass. If East had passed, you would have had to bid one spade. Now that East has bid one heart you are no longer forced to bid. Any action by you in this situation constitutes a "free" bid and shows some values. Holding the hand in Example 1, you'd bid one spade here.

Example 4.
As South you hold ♠ A Q 6 4 2  ♡ 7 4  ◊ K J 8
♣ 8 3 2.   The bidding goes

| WEST | NORTH | EAST | SOUTH |
|------|-------|------|-------|
| 1 ♡ | Double | Pass | ? |

What do you bid? The answer is two spades. With 10 high-card points and a good suit, a jump bid is in order. Most experts don't play this jump as forcing. It's very encouraging, however, and partner will pass only if his take-out double was a dead minimum.

Example 5.
As South you hold ♠ 10 5 4 2  ♡ A 5  ◊ A K 7
♣ K 6 3 2.   The bidding goes

| WEST | NORTH | EAST | SOUTH |
|------|-------|------|-------|
| 1 ♡ | Double | Pass | ? |

What do you bid? The answer is two hearts. Game is assured, but you are not certain where. A cue bid in the opponent's suit here simply means, "I have a very good hand, partner, but I'd like you to pick the suit."

Example 6.
As South you hold  ♠ 6 5 2  ♡ J 8  ♢ K J 10 7  ♣ A 10 8 2.   The bidding goes

| WEST | NORTH | EAST | SOUTH |
|------|-------|------|-------|
| 1 ♢ | Double | Pass | ? |

What do you bid? The answer is one no-trump. A response of one no-trump to a take-out double shows about 8 or 9 points and the opponent's suit well stopped.

Example 7.
As South you hold  ♠ K Q 8 6 4 2  ♡ 8 4 3  ♢ K J 3  ♣ 2.   The bidding goes

| WEST | NORTH | EAST | SOUTH |
|------|-------|------|-------|
| 1 ♡ | Double | Pass | ? |

What do you bid? The answer is four spades. Opposite partner's double you want to play this hand in four spades, so go ahead and bid it.

### After Partner Responds to Your Take-out Double

When partner responds to your take-out double, always bear in mind that you *forced* him to bid. Let's suppose the bidding goes

| EAST | SOUTH | WEST | NORTH |
|------|-------|------|-------|
| 1 ♣ | Double | Pass | 1 ♠ |
| Pass | ? | | |

As South, what do you do next with each of the following hands?

Example 1.
♠ A J 8   ♡ K Q 5 3   ◇ Q J 5 3   ♣ 9 7

You should pass. You have bid every value in your hand when you doubled. Your partner will be disappointed at your spade holding. He was hoping for four-card support. Remember, partner may have nothing, in which case he's going to have trouble even making one spade.

Example 2.
♠ A 10 9 2   ♡ K Q 5 4   ◇ K Q 5 4   ♣ 4

Bid two spades. You have more than you promised with the double. If partner holds a maximum, such as ♠ K 5 4 3   ♡ J 8   ◇ A 9 8 3   ♣ 8 6 5, he'll carry on to game, which should be made. And even if partner has nothing, you should be safe at the two level.

Example 3.
♠ A J 8 3   ♡ K Q 10 6   ◇ K Q J 7   ♣ 4

Bid three spades. Partner will pass with a hand like ♠ Q 10 6 2   ♡ 9 4 3   ◇ 9 8 2   ♣ 10 8 3. He'll bid four spades if he holds ♠ Q 7 6 2   ♡ A 8 2   ◇ 9 8 2 ♣ 10 8 3.

Example 4.
♠ K J 8 3   ♡ A K Q 3   ◇ K Q J 10   ◇ 4

Bid four spades. It's true that your partner may go down if he holds as little as ♠ 9 7 6 4   ♡ 7 6   ◇ 7 4 3 ♣ 10 8 3 2,   but you cannot base your bids on such a pessimistic assumption. It's more realistic to assume that your partner has something like ♠ Q 10 5 4   ♡ 7 6 ◇ 7 4 3   ♣ 10 8 3 2.   You should act accordingly.

## After an Opponent's Take-out Double

When your right-hand opponent doubles your partner's opening bid, your action should be governed by one very simple rule: *With 10 or more high-card points, redouble!* With less than 10 high-card points, make your natural call.

Suppose the bidding goes

| NORTH | EAST |
|-------|------|
| 1 ♠ | Double |

As South, what do you do with each of the following hands?

Example 1.
♠ 8    ♡ K Q 10 6    ◇ A J 9 6    ♣ K 10 8 2

You should redouble. Next round you plan to double anything the opponents bid. Don't worry about the single-ton spade. It's practically impossible for the opponents to pass one spade redoubled, and even if they did, partner would surely make seven tricks on power alone.

Example 2.
♠ K 8 7 3    ♡ 6 4    ◇ A 10 9 4    ♣ A Q 5

Redouble. Next round you plan to jump to three spades. After your redouble, any jump or new suit by you is forcing. If you don't redouble, nothing you do is forcing.

Example 3.
♠ K J 8 6    ♡ 7 5    ◇ 10 9 3 2    ♣ 9 5 4

Bid two spades. A single raise here is apt to be a little weaker than if East had not doubled. Your raise may keep West out of the auction. Or if the opponents get to game, it may allow your partner to make a good sacrifice.

Example 4.
♠ K J 8 2    ♡ 6 5    ◇ K Q 4 3    ♣ 9 6 2

Bid three spades. You've denied holding 10 high-card points by not redoubling, so the jump is not forcing. The jump raise over a take-out double resembles a very strong single raise under normal circumstances.

Example 5.
♠ K J 8 5 4   ♡ 6   ◇ Q J 8 5 4   ♣ 9 2

Bid four spades just as you would without the double.

Example 6.
♠ J 8   ♡ A J 8   ◇ Q J 7 3   ♣ 8 5 3 2

Bid one no-trump. A response of one no-trump normally shows 6 to 9 points. Over a take-out double, however, it is dangerous to bid one no-trump with a minimum. Thus a response of one no-trump over a take-out double tends to show 8 or 9 points and, of course, balanced distribution.

Example 7.
♠ 9 2   ♡ Q 6 3 2   ◇ J 9 5 4 2   ♣ 6 5

The way to show you have nothing is to pass.

Example 8.
♠ 9 4   ♡ Q 5   ◇ K Q 10 7 6 4   ♣ J 4 2

Bid two diamonds. A new suit after a take-out double is not forcing because you have denied 10 high-card points by your failure to redouble.

**The Double of an Opening One No-Trump Bid**

Although the double of an opening suit bid is for take-out, the double of an opening one no-trump bid is primarily for penalties. The doubler shows 16 or more points, and his partner is expected to pass unless he has good reason to remove the double.

Suppose the bidding goes

| WEST | NORTH | EAST | SOUTH |
|------|-------|------|-------|
| 1 NT | Double | Pass | ? |

As South you should pass if you hold something like
♠ K 4 3   ♡ 9 4 3 2   ◇ Q 10 9   ♣ 9 8 2. Your 5
points added to partner's minimum of 16 points give your
side more points than the opponents. You will probably
beat one no-trump. Even with a worthless balanced hand
it is usually best to pass. With a long suit, however, it's
best to run. Holding a hand like   ♠ J 8 6 5 3 2   ♡ 9 2
◇ 8 7 6   ♣ 5 4   you should bid two spades.

## The Double of an Opening Suit Bid of More Than One

The double of any opening suit bid from one club
through four hearts is primarily for take-out. A double of
four spades is for penalties. (Over four spades a bid of
four no-trump is for take-out.) Naturally, there are degrees of emphasis in a take-out double depending on the
level. Thus the higher the bid, the more often your partner
will be able to leave in the double.

You must *always* take out partner's double of an opening suit bid at the one level, except on the very rare occasion when you hold something like K Q J 10 x x of trumps.

The double of a weak two-bid should be treated in
almost the same manner as the double of a one-bid. Suppose the bidding goes

| WEST | NORTH | EAST | SOUTH |
|------|-------|------|-------|
| 2 ♡ | Double | Pass | ? |

As South you hold   ♠ 10 9 7 6   ♡ Q 10 6 5   ◇ A 5
♣ 5 3 2.   Your correct bid is two spades. If you held
♠ 10 6 5   ♡ Q J 10 8 4   ◇ A 4   ♣ 5 3 2   then you
should accept the responsibility of passing the double.
(Notice that this trump holding is not quite good enough
to pass a double of one heart. Over one heart doubled,
South should respond one no-trump with this hand.)

97

At the three level, the double is still primarily for take-out. Suppose neither side is vulnerable and the bidding goes

| WEST | NORTH | EAST | SOUTH |
|------|-------|------|-------|
| 3 ♡ | Double | Pass | ? |

As South you hold ♠ K J 7 6  ♡ Q 9 8 5  ◊ 6 2 ♣ J 7 3. Your correct bid is three spades. If you held ♠ A 4 2  ♡ Q J 10 8  ◊ 6 4 2  ♣ J 8 7 you should pass.

Of course it's easier to leave in the double at the four level. Suppose the bidding goes

| WEST | NORTH | EAST | SOUTH |
|------|-------|------|-------|
| 4 ♡ | Double | Pass | ? |

As South you hold ♠ Q J 9 6 5  ♡ 6 2  ◊ J 8 ♣ K Q 6 2. Your correct bid is four spades. However, if you held ♠ K 9 6  ♡ J 10 9 6  ◊ Q 5 4  ♣ J 8 4, you should pass. You have no place to go.


## How Much Strength Do You Need to Double an Opening Suit Bid of More Than One?

With the right shape, all you need is a sound opening bid. Holding ♠ A J 10 6  ♡ 6  ◊ K J 10 2 ♣ K Q 9 7 I would double any opening heart bid regardless of the level. It's true that on the rare occasion when my partner has a bust we're going to be in trouble. In the long run, however, the double will pay off.


## Other Take-out Doubles

In addition to the double of opening suit bids, there are many other situations where a double is for take-out. How can you tell whether it's for take-out or penalties? A very general rule is the following: Almost any double of a suit contract is primarily for take-out *provided that the doubler's partner has never bid.*

Example 1.

| SOUTH | WEST | NORTH | EAST |
|-------|------|-------|------|
| 1 ♡ | Double | 2 ♡ | Pass |
| Pass | Double | | |

West's double is still for take-out because his partner has never bid.

Example 2.

| SOUTH | WEST | NORTH | EAST |
|-------|------|-------|------|
| 1 ◇ | 1 ♡ | Pass | 3 ♡ |
| Double | | | |

South's double is for take-out because North has never bid. South probably holds something like  ♠ A J 9 7  ♡ 5  ◇ A K J 3  ♣ K Q 5 3.

Example 3.

| SOUTH | WEST | NORTH | EAST |
|-------|------|-------|------|
| 1 ♡ | Pass | 1 ♠ | 2 ♣ |
| Double | | | |

Here South's double is for penalties because his partner has made a bid. South may hold something like  ♠ 8  ♡ A K J 6 3  ◇ K 9 6  ♣ A J 9 7.

Exception:

| SOUTH | WEST | NORTH | EAST |
|-------|------|-------|------|
| 1 ♡ | Pass | 1 ♠ | Pass |
| 2 ♡ | Double | | |

On this sequence, West is doubling for penalties even though his partner has never bid. The reason is that if West had a take-out double, he would have doubled South's one-heart bid. The only excuse for passing over one heart and doubling now is that West has a strong hand with long hearts.

## The Balance

The art of reopening a dead auction is called balancing. Consider the following bidding:

| WEST | NORTH | EAST | SOUTH |
|------|-------|------|-------|
| 1 ♠ | Pass | Pass | ? |

In a good bridge game, South will seldom pass this sequence. As East-West have died at one spade, it's very likely that North-South have at least half the high-card strength. Why should South sell out for one spade when his side can probably score at least a partial instead? It requires substantially less strength to balance than to act in the immediate seat because the balancer knows from his opponents' bidding that his partner holds some cards.

In the auction shown above, what should South do with each of the following hands:

### Example 1.

♠ 7 2 ♡ A Q 9 6 4 ◇ Q J 4 ♣ 9 8 2. The answer is bid two hearts. This hand is not good enough to bid two hearts immediately over a one-spade bid. When the bidding has died, however, it is safe to bid two hearts, because North is now marked with some values.

### Example 2.

♠ A Q 4 ♡ K 8 6 ◇ Q J 9 7 ♣ J 10 2. You should bid one no-trump. In the balancing seat, one no-trump shows about an ace or a king less than an ordinary one no-trump overcall.

### Example 3.

♠ A Q 6 ♡ K J 8 ◇ K J 10 9 ♣ K 9 5. You should double with this hand. You have too much to bid one no-trump in the balancing seat. You must double first and then bid no-trump next round.

Example 4.
♠ Q 10 9 6 5  ♡ 8  ◇ 9 8  ♣ A K J 10 5.  You should
pass. Don't balance when you have the opponent's suit.
Just pass and take a small profit. If you bid two clubs,
East and West may find a better spot.

Example 5.
♠ 9 6  ♡ A 9 8 2  ◇ K 9 8 6  ♣ K J 10.  You should
double. You don't have quite enough for an immediate
double of one spade, but in the balancing seat the double
is correct.

In all cases the partner of the balancer must refrain
from becoming unduly excited by his own high cards. He
must remember that partner took most of them into account when he balanced. Consider the following bidding:

| WEST | NORTH | EAST | SOUTH |
|------|-------|------|-------|
| 1 ♡ | Pass | 2 ♡ | Pass |
| Pass | 2 ♠ | Pass | Pass |
| 3 ♡ | Pass | Pass | ? |

As South you hold  ♠ A 8 4  ♡ K J 6  ◇ 9 8 5 4
♣ K 8 6.  You should pass. Partner has already bid your
cards when he balanced. North and South have achieved
their aim by forcing East and West up to the three level
where they may be set. Don't press your luck with a second
balance. One balance a hand is usually enough.

Another indispensable tool of the balancer is the "unusual no-trump." For a discussion of this, see Chapter 11,
"The Gadgets."

## Wriggling and the S.O.S. Redouble

Even experts sometimes land in the soup. As a general
rule when this happens the best policy is to lie still and
take your licking. Any attempt to climb out usually makes
matters much worse. Consider this bidding:

| WEST | NORTH | EAST | SOUTH |
|------|-------|------|-------|
| 1 ♠ | 2 ♡ | Double | ? |

As South you hold  ♠ Q 7 6   ♡ 6   ◇ A Q 7 5 3 2
♣ 9 7 6.  It looks as though partner is in trouble. Nevertheless, the right action is to pass. If you run to three
diamonds, and partner doesn't have diamonds, you will
have escaped from a small disaster at two hearts doubled,
to wind up in a massacre at three diamonds doubled.
Don't rescue partner unless you have a safe landing spot.
It would be proper to run to three diamonds if you held a
hand like ♠ Q 5 4  ♡ —  ◇ Q J 10 9 7 6 4  ♣ J 6 5.

Occasionally when you're in trouble, you'll be in the
position of knowing that a sanctuary exists, but not knowing where. Consider this bidding:

| NORTH | EAST | SOUTH | WEST |
|-------|------|-------|------|
| 1 ◇ | Pass | Pass | Double |
| Pass | Pass | ? | |

As South you hold  ♠ J 9 6 5   ♡ 9 8 4 2   ◇ 7
♣ 10 6 4 3.  One diamond doubled is sure to be disastrous. With this hand, weak as it is, you very likely have
a better fit somewhere else. The problem is to find it.
When a partnership is in trouble, a redouble by the player
in the *last* seat is usually an S.O.S. If you have a good
partner, you should redouble, forcing him to run.

Here is a similar situation:

| SOUTH | WEST | NORTH | EAST |
|-------|------|-------|------|
| 1 ♣ | Double | Pass | Pass |
| ? | | | |

As South you hold  ♠ A 7 4 3   ♡ K 8 6   ◇ K 9 4
♣ A 4 2.  Obviously you are in the wrong contract.
Rather than fumble around yourself trying to land on your
feet, the best procedure with a good partner is to redouble
for S.O.S. Partner will bid his longest suit and you'll probably be out of the woods.

Notice that if the bidding goes

| SOUTH | WEST | NORTH | EAST |
|-------|------|-------|------|
| 1 ♣ | Double | Pass | Pass |

and you are fortunate enough to hold  ♠ A K  ♡ 8 7 4
♢ A K 2  ♣ K Q 9 8 5,  you must pass. One club doubled is a very pleasant spot. To redouble here would be the height of greed. You'll never get to play one club redoubled. Either your partner will rescue you or an opponent will run. Moral: Don't redouble in the last seat when you're happy with your contract.

Don't confuse the immediate redouble with the S.O.S. redouble. For example,

| SOUTH | WEST | NORTH | EAST |
|-------|------|-------|------|
| 1 ♡ | Pass | Pass | Double |
| Redouble | | | |

In this case, South is not asking partner to run. A redouble in the immediate seat simply shows a very strong hand. South could hold something like  ♠ K 9  ♡ A K J 8 6
♢ A K 8  ♣ J 6 2.

There is one situation, however, where many experts use the S.O.S. redouble in the immediate seat. Consider this bidding:

| WEST | NORTH | EAST | SOUTH |
|------|-------|------|-------|
| 1 ♠ | 2 ♣ | Double | Redouble |

It makes no sense to use the redouble here to announce to the world that you expect to take at least eight tricks at clubs. It is more valuable to use the redouble for a hand such as  ♠ A 6 5  ♡ Q J 10 8 6  ♢ Q 10 9 7 5
♣ —.  You are in grave jeopardy at two clubs doubled, and will almost certainly find a haven if partner runs.

Warning: The S.O.S. redouble is extremely dangerous. Never use it with a bad partner because he may leave it in and you'll be slaughtered. Even with an expert partner, you should never use the S.O.S. redouble in the immediate seat unless you have specifically discussed the matter with him previously.

**Forcing and Nonforcing Situations in Defensive Bidding**

A jump raise of an overcall is strong but not forcing.

| WEST | NORTH | EAST | SOUTH |
|---|---|---|---|
| 1 ♡ | 1 ♠ | Pass | 3 ♠ |

South's jump raise to three spades strongly invites a game, and takes into account the vulnerability. If the partnership is vulnerable, North should be close to an opening bid and South might have ♠ K 8 6 5 ♡ 4 3 ◇ A J 9 7 ♣ Q J 9. Not vulnerable, the overcaller might be weaker, and the responder would therefore need to be slightly stronger. With a better hand, such as ♠ K 8 6 5 4 ♡ 3 ◇ A J 9 7 ♣ Q J 9, South should jump to four spades.

A new suit in response to an overcall is also not forcing.

| WEST | NORTH | EAST | SOUTH |
|---|---|---|---|
| 1 ◇ | 1 ♠ | Pass | 2 ♡ |

South could hold ♠ 5 4 ♡ A Q J 8 5 3 ◇ 6 2 ♣ Q 9 7. North is at liberty to pass. The accepted method of forcing in this situation is to use a cue bid of two diamonds. This cue bid in the opponent's suit simply says, "Partner, I have a very strong hand but I am not sure where we belong."

Summing up: In most auctions the side that opens the bidding has an advantage. Against average players this advantage is very large because the average player is weak in defensive bidding. Expert players can usually overcome the initial advantage of the opening bid by judicious use of the standard defensive weapons discussed in this chapter.

# 10

# Advanced Bidding

There are certain bids that give partner a precise picture of your hand and may therefore be referred to as "limit bids." These include no-trump bids, pre-emptive bids, raises of partner's suit, and to a lesser extent rebids of your own suit. Other bids are relatively unlimited because their range of meaning is so wide. Obviously, when you have a choice between the two, it is wiser to choose the limit bid. For example, if you hold ♠ A Q  ♡ K J 9 ◊ K J 9 6 2  ♣ Q 10 5  it would not be *wrong* to open one diamond, but it would be *inferior*. The limit bid of one no-trump is superior.

As soon as one player makes a limit bid his partner is in the best position to judge the final contract and therefore automatically becomes captain for the rest of the auction.

Example:

| | WEST | | EAST |
|---|---|---|---|
| ♠ | J 8 | ♠ | K Q 10 9 6 5 |
| ♡ | A J 10 8 3 | ♡ | 7 2 |
| ◊ | K 9 3 | ◊ | Q J 10 |
| ♣ | K J 8 | ♣ | A 3 |

The bidding proceeds as follows:

| WEST | EAST |
|------|------|
| 1 ♡ | 1 ♠ |
| 1 NT | 4 ♠ |

West's one-heart bid is unlimited. It simply shows a hand somewhere in the 12-to-20-point range with almost any distribution that includes four or more hearts.

East's one-spade bid is even more unlimited. He is probably in the 6-to-18-point range with almost any distribution including four or more spades.

West's one no-trump rebid, however, is a limit bid. It shows precisely 12 to 15 high-card points and balanced distribution.

East is now the captain. He knows the partnership has sufficient assets to make a game but not a slam, and he knows the partnership has at least eight spades. No further investigation is necessary, and he bids a game in spades.

It's not always possible to make a limit bid early in the auction. In a bidding sequence such as

| WEST | EAST |
|------|------|
| 1 ♠ | 2 ◇ |
| 2 ♡ | 3 ♣ |

all the bids are virtually unlimited.

In an unlimited auction there is no captain. The further the bidding advances without a captain the more hazardous is the outcome. It's as though two people set out to sea in a small boat, each determined to steer in his own direction. The sooner they elect a captain the more successful their journey will be.

Some players, even some very good players, are individualists who hate to turn over control of the auction to their partners. They deliberately avoid making a limit bid in hopes that partner will limit his hand first.

Example:
East holds &spades; A J 7  &hearts; Q 5 3  &diams; K J 8 5  &clubs; A J 8.

The bidding:

| WEST | EAST |
|------|------|
| 1 &hearts; | ? |

East has a clear-cut three no-trump bid showing 16 or 17 points, very balanced distribution (almost always 4–3–3–3), and all unbid suits stopped. If East is an individualist, however, he won't bid three no-trump, because he doesn't trust his partner to know what to do next. Instead he tries to feel out his partner by bidding two diamonds. Two diamonds is not a "wrong" bid, but it is an *inferior* bid. East will never get another chance to describe this hand so precisely.

The worst bidding sequences occur when two individualists are partners and neither wants to elect the other fellow captain. They manufacture suits as they go along, and are constantly on the brink of disaster. Even if they land on their feet at the last minute, what advantage have they gained by doing things the hard way?

It is very difficult to place the final contract with any degree of accuracy until one player makes a limit bid. Once a limit bid is made, however, the partnership will usually have smooth sailing.

If the captain can't place the contract immediately, he may conduct a short investigation or he may conduct a very refined investigation, depending on the circumstances.

Example:

| WEST | EAST |
|------|------|
| &spades; A K 9 4 3 | &spades; Q J 6 5 |
| &hearts; A 3 2 | &hearts; 9 7 |
| &diams; A 7 5 3 | &diams; 8 6 2 |
| &clubs; 9 | &clubs; K J 4 3 |

The bidding:

| WEST | EAST |
|------|------|
| 1 &spades; | 2 &spades; |
| 3 &diams; | 3 &spades; |
| Pass | |

East's two-spade raise has limited his hand, and West is now the captain. He can see that game is likely, depending on the quality of partner's raise. He could make a general-direction shot of three spades at this point, in which case East would pass with a minimum and carry on with a maximum. With West's actual hand, it is better to make the more specific game try of three diamonds. (Remember, once a trump suit has been agreed upon, any new suit is forcing.) Three diamonds here asks East in evaluating his hand to pay special attention to his diamond holding. East makes the minimum rebid of three spades. His raise was only fair to begin with. Now, in the light of his unfavorable diamond holding, it has to be considerably devalued. Give East ♠ Q 8 6 3   ♡ 9 7   ◇ K Q 2 ♣ 9 7 4 2   and he would jump to four spades over West's three diamond bid, because he'd know his diamond honors were worth their weight in gold.

In slam bidding the same general principles apply. However, as slams usually depend on aces and kings, the emphasis here is on showing specific controls.

Example:

| | WEST | EAST |
|---|---|---|
| ♠ | A 10 6 5 3 2 | K J 8 7 |
| ♡ | K Q 2 | A J 10 8 |
| ◇ | 6 | Q 8 7 |
| ♣ | A J 5 | K 8 |

The bidding:

| WEST | EAST |
|---|---|
| 1 ♠ | 3 ♠ |
| 4 ♣ | 4 ♡ |
| 6 ♠ | |

Again East has limited his hand, this time with a jump raise. West is now the captain. He knows the partnership values are approaching the slam zone and he makes a slam try of four clubs. East cooperates in the slam effort by showing the heart ace, and West is now able to bid six spades.

If East had a minimum for his previous bidding, he would not cooperate in the slam effort. For example, if East had held ♠ Q J 8 7 ♡ A J 8 7 ◊ Q J 6 ♣ Q 8 he would still have bid three spades in response to West's one-spade opening. Over four clubs, however, he would not encourage partner by showing the heart ace. He would simply sign off by bidding four spades.

Here is a more advanced example:

|  | WEST | EAST |
|---|---|---|
| ♠ | K Q 8 7 4 2 | A J 10 5 |
| ♡ | A 3 | Q 8 4 |
| ◊ | A | K Q 5 2 |
| ♣ | A Q 7 6 | K 8 |

The bidding:

| WEST | EAST |
|---|---|
| 1 ♠ | 3 ♠ |
| 4 ♣ | 5 ♣ |
| 7 ♠ | |

In this case, East has a difficult choice after partner's four-club bid. His three-spade bid was a maximum, so he does not want to rebid four spades. A simple return to the agreed trump suits is always reserved to show minimum values. He can't bid four diamonds because he doesn't have the diamond ace; and he can't bid four hearts because he doesn't have the heart ace. A straightforward jump to six spades would not be wrong, but an even better bid is five clubs, showing partner the club king as well as strong interests in slam proceedings. Five clubs is just what West wanted to hear, and he is now able to bid the grand slam. Note that West is not at all worried about the ace of spades. He knows partner couldn't make such an aggressive call as five clubs on an ace-less hand and with no high honor in trumps.

In each of the above examples, the limit bid was in the form of a raise in partner's suit. If the limit bid is in no-trump, the trump suit will sometimes be agreed upon by inference.

Example:

| | WEST | | EAST |
|---|---|---|---|
| ♠ | K J 8 2 | ♠ | A Q 10 6 5 |
| ♡ | A 10 9 | ♡ | K Q 4 |
| ◊ | K Q 5 2 | ◊ | — |
| ♣ | A 3 | ♣ | K Q J 8 6 |

The bidding:

| WEST | EAST |
|---|---|
| 1 NT | 3 ♠ |
| 4 ♣ | 4 ◊ |
| 4 ♡ | 7 ♠ |

As soon as West bids one no-trump, East becomes captain. He knows there is a slam, but he's not sure whether spades or clubs would be the best suit. He investigates spades first by bidding three spades. He knows his partner will bid three no-trump with only a doubleton spade, in which case he plans to bid the slam in clubs.

With three or more spades, West would normally raise three spades to four. With this super-fit, however, he makes a bid which is even stronger than four spades. He bids four clubs, which says, "Partner, you really hit me. I have excellent support, a maximum no-trump in terms of useful cards for you, and incidentally the ace of clubs." The four-club cue bid agrees upon spades by *inference*. By the way, West chooses to show the club ace rather than the heart ace to conserve bidding space in case East wants to investigate further.

East is delighted to learn partner has such good spade support and he is especially pleased about the club ace. If partner has the heart ace too, East wants to bid a grand slam in spades. So he bids four diamonds to make it convenient for West to show the heart ace if he has it. West shows the heart ace and East can bid seven spades.

Sometimes the captain will strike gold with his second suit.

Example:

|  | WEST | EAST |
|---|---|---|
| ♠ | K J | A Q 9 7 5 |
| ♡ | A J 6 | 7 2 |
| ◇ | K 10 9 6 | A J 8 7 2 |
| ♣ | A 10 7 4 | 6 |

The bidding:

| WEST | EAST |
|---|---|
| 1 NT | 3 ♠ |
| 3 NT | 4 ◇ |
| 4 ♡ | 6 ◇ |

Again, East becomes captain as soon as West opens with one no-trump. He bids three spades hoping to interest partner in the spade suit. But partner has only two spades so he returns to three no-trump. When East bids four diamonds, however, West perks up. He has excellent diamond support and all key cards on the side. A simple raise to five diamonds would be an underbid. He tells partner that he has a super diamond raise by showing him the heart ace, and East gladly bids six diamonds.

Here is a different kind of situation, with an intervening bid by an opponent:

|  | WEST | EAST |
|---|---|---|
| ♠ | K Q 8 7 5 4 | A J 3 2 |
| ♡ | 9 6 | J 7 2 |
| ◇ | A | K Q J 5 |
| ♣ | A K 4 3 | Q J |

The bidding:

| WEST | NORTH | EAST | SOUTH |
|---|---|---|---|
| 1 ♠ | 2 ♡ | 3 ♠ | Pass |
| 5 ♠ | Pass | Pass | Pass |

West knows the partnership may have sufficient assets to make a slam as soon as he hears partner's three-spade bid. His only concern is the opponent's suit. Rather than cue bid his aces one at a time, he can get his message across in one bid. A jump to five spades in this situation says, "We are in the slam zone, partner, but I'm worried about the heart suit." East does not have heart control either, so he has to pass. If East had held ♠ A J 3 2 ♡ 7 ◇ K Q J 5 ♣ Q J 7 5 he would, of course, bid six spades.

## QUIZ ON CAPTAIN-AND-CREW PROBLEMS

Test yourself and see how helpful a partner you are. In each of the following sequences you have already limited your hand. Partner is now the captain and he's asking you for further information. What do you bid?

The bidding:

| PARTNER | YOU |
|---------|-----|
| 1 ♡ | 2 ♡ |
| 3 ♣ | ? |

You hold:
1. ♠ 8 6　♡ K Q 3 2　◇ J 4 3　♣ 9 7 5 4
2. ♠ A J 9　♡ K 9 6　◇ J 10 5 4 2　♣ 5 4
3. ♠ 9 6 4　♡ 10 9 8 2　◇ A 5 4 2　♣ K 4
4. ♠ A 6　♡ J 10 5 4　◇ A 7 5 4　♣ 8 4 3

The bidding:

| PARTNER | YOU |
|---------|-----|
| 1 ♡ | 3 ♡ |
| 3 ♠ | ? |

You hold:
5. ♠ K 8　♡ A 10 7 5　◇ K 9 3 2　♣ A J 6
6. ♠ Q J 8　♡ K J 8 4　◇ J 8　♣ A 6 4 2

The bidding:

|  | PARTNER | YOU |
|---|---|---|
|  | 1 ♠ | 2 NT |
|  | 3 ♡ | ? |

You hold:

7. ♠ Q 6 5　♡ A 8 6　◇ A 9 8　♣ K 10 9 8
8. ♠ J 5 2　♡ K J 8 2　◇ A Q 5　♣ Q J 8
9. ♠ Q J 3　♡ K J 4　◇ A 9 6 5　♣ A 8 4
10. ♠ 9 8　♡ K J 8　◇ A Q 8 7　♣ K J 9 8

The bidding:

|  | YOU | PARTNER |
|---|---|---|
|  | 1 ♡ | 2 ◇ |
|  | 2 ♡ | 2 ♠ |
|  | ? |  |

You hold:

11. ♠ A 4　♡ K Q J 9 8 6 2　◇ Q 5　♣ J 8

The bidding:

|  | YOU | PARTNER |
|---|---|---|
|  | 3 ♡ | 3 ♠ |
|  | ? |  |

You hold:

12. ♠ Q 3 2　♡ A Q J 10 8 7 2　◇ 6　♣ 9 8

**Answers to Quiz**

1. Three hearts. When you bid two hearts you showed partner a hand worth 6 to 10 points in support of hearts. This is a minimum, and the way to show you have a minimum is simply to return to the agreed trump suit.
2. Three no-trump. This is a maximum raise. However, it would be wrong to jump to four hearts with only three trumps. The solution is to bid three no-trump,

showing partner that your original raise was sound (although probably based on only three trumps) and that you have stoppers in the unbid suits.

3. Four hearts. Although you have only seven points in high cards, this hand will be very welcome to partner. Your club holding is particularly attractive opposite his three-club try. And, of course, an ace is always useful.

4. Four hearts. Even though your club holding is poor, it is right to jump to four hearts on this super maximum.

5. Four clubs. You have already announced a hand worth 13 to 16 points in support of hearts, and partner has made a slam try. As you have a maximum, particularly in terms of aces and kings, you should cooperate with his slam effort and show the ace of clubs.

6. Four hearts. You have a minimum so you must try to slow your partner down by returning to the agreed trump suit.

7. Three spades. You have shown 13 to 15 high-card points and stoppers in hearts, diamonds, and clubs. Now partner has asked you to choose between spades and hearts. With three of each you naturally take him back to his first suit.

8. Four hearts. With four cards in partner's second suit it's correct to raise him to four hearts.

9. Four spades. If you bid only three spades with this hand, partner would expect something like Example 7. This time you have "magic cards" for partner. Every honor you have is working. Remember, aces are always useful. Kings, queens, and jacks can be wasted opposite partner's short suits, but are priceless opposite partner's long suits. If partner holds something like ♠ A K 9 8 2  ♡ Q 9 8 6 3  ◊ K 2 ♣ 3,  you belong in a slam. You must alert partner to the excellent fit by jumping to four spades.

10. Three no-trump. This usually means you don't have three spades or four hearts, and that you have both diamonds and clubs doubly stopped.

11. Four hearts, although your hand is in the minimum opening-bid range, the texture of your heart suit is excellent. The hand will play well in hearts even without trump support from partner. You have already announced you were in the minimum class with your first rebid of two hearts. By jumping to four hearts now, you show the powerful heart suit.

12. Four spades. Again, you have limited your hand, this time with an opening pre-empt of three hearts. Partner is now captain and his three-spade bid is, of course, forcing (new suit by responder). You have very suitable support for spades considering your original pre-empt, so the proper bid is four spades.

## Limit Raises

Tournament players, playing in fixed partnerships, often introduce exceptions to the basic rule that jump bids by the responder are forcing. The most common of these is in this sequence:

| NORTH | SOUTH |
|-------|-------|
| 1 ♡ | 3 ♡ |

The standard meaning of this bid is of course that South has an opening bid with 13-16 points and is promising a game. The alternative is called a "limit raise," in which case three hearts invites a game but does not guarantee it. South would have the equivalent of 10-12 points.

Example:
♠ A Q   ♡ K J 5 4   ◇ 8 7 4 2   ♣ J 5 2

This would be difficult to bid in response to one heart playing normal methods. It is ideally suited to a limit raise of three hearts, allowing partner to pass if he has a minimum.

This raises an obvious question: What should responder do when playing limit raises if his hand is suitable for traditional forcing raise? Many players by agreement use three no-trump for this purpose, giving up the use of this bid to show 16 or 17 points and a balanced hand. Alternatively the opener can bid a new suit and then jump to game in opener's suit. (See also "Splinter Bids" in Chapter 15.)

The limit raise idea can logically be extended to the second round of the bidding:

| NORTH | SOUTH |
|-------|-------|
| 1 ♣ | 1 ◊ |
| 1 ♡ | 3 ♡ |

South could have the hand shown above. A raise to four hearts would be stronger, promising four-card support and an opening bid; not the same at all as a first-round raise to four hearts, which would *deny* an opening bid.

## Cue-Bid in the Opponents' Suit

If a beginner had the opportunity to kibitz a game, and wanted to judge the level of expertise of the players who were watching, he could apply a simple numerical test. He would have to count the number of times somebody bid a suit that had already been bid by an opponent. Experts do this very frequently. Beginners hardly ever.

At a high-level, when a suit has been agreed, this is like any of the cue-bids already discussed in this chapter; a move toward slam showing control of the suit bid.

Much more common and important is the cue-bid at a low level. This simply indicates a desire to reach game, and asks partner to continue in some intelligent fashion. It does *not* promise any control of the enemy suit.

This can occur in a wide variety of situations. Here we have space only for some of the most common.

| A. | NORTH | EAST |
|----|-------|------|
| | 1 ♡ | 2 ♡ |

East must have a monster hand on which he would have opened with a strong two-bid if given the chance: ♠ A K Q 4 3   ♡ 5 2   ◊ A K J 5 3 2   ♣ —   for example.

However, such monster hands are very rare in the face of opening bid, so many tournament players use this particular cue-bid conventionally to show some kind of two-suited hand. The most popular version is "Michaels," in which the cue-bidder shows both major suits if the opening bid was a minor, or a major and a minor if the opening bid was a major.

B.

| NORTH | EAST | SOUTH | WEST |
|-------|------|-------|------|
| 1 ♡ | Double | Pass | 2 ♣ |
| Pass | 2 ♡ | | |

West was forced to respond to the double and may have no high-card strength at all. In spite of this, East is still interested in game. He must have an enormous hand, probably with 20 high-card points or more. Example: ♠ A K J 5   ♡ 3   ◊ A K Q 4 2   ♣ K 6 4. West must bid, and can afford to bid strongly if he has five points or more.

C.

| NORTH | EAST | SOUTH |
|-------|------|-------|
| 1 ♡ | 2 ♣ | 3 ♣ |

South promises a heart fit and an opening bid. This is particularly useful for players using the limit raises described earlier in this chapter, for the cue-bid now shows a strong raise. Example: ♠ 6 5   ♡ K J 8 4   ◊ A J 5   ♣ A 6 5 2.   The partnership will certainly reach a game and perhaps a slam.

D.

| NORTH | EAST | SOUTH | WEST |
|-------|------|-------|------|
| 1 ♣ | 1 ♠ | Pass | 2 ♣ |

West has a strong hand, equivalent to an opening bid or better, and is hoping to reach a game. He might have

♠ K 5  ♡ A Q 6 3 2  ◇ A J 7 5  ♣ 6 2.  It would
be a bad mistake for him to bid two hearts with this hand,
since this would not be forcing. Remember that new suit
bids are never forcing if the opponents have opened the
bidding.

In the chapter on competitive bidding we had a similar
example of the use of the cue-bid in response to a take-out
double.

Keep looking for opportunities to use the low-level cue-
bid, showing a strong desire to reach game and lack of
any other bid to describe the hand. You will be surprised
how many you will find.

However there is one exception. If a player unexpect-
edly bids the opponents' suit after he and his partner both
passed on the previous round, the bid is natural.

| NORTH | EAST | SOUTH | WEST |
|-------|------|-------|------|
| 1 ◇ | Pass | 1 ♡ | Pass |
| 1 ♠ | 2 ◇ | | |

If East had a strong hand he would have bid the first
time. So he must have a long strong diamond suit.


## QUIZ ON CUE-BIDDING

In each of the bidding sequences shown you are South.
Decide the meaning of your partner's final bid.

| 1. | EAST | SOUTH | WEST | NORTH |
|----|------|-------|------|-------|
| | 1 ♡ | Dbl. | 2 ♡ | 3 ♡ |

| 2. | SOUTH | WEST | NORTH | |
|----|-------|------|-------|--|
| | 1 NT | 2 ♡ | 3 ♡ | |

| 3. | EAST | SOUTH | WEST | NORTH |
|----|------|-------|------|-------|
| | 1 ♡ | Pass | 1 ♠ | Pass |
| | 2 ♣ | Pass | Pass | 2 ♠ |

| 4. | EAST | SOUTH | WEST | NORTH |
|----|------|-------|------|-------|
|    | 3 ◇  | Dbl.  | Pass | 4 ◇   |

| 5. | NORTH | EAST | SOUTH | WEST |
|----|-------|------|-------|------|
|    | 1 ♡   | 2 ♣  | 3 ♡   | Pass |
|    | 4 ♣   |      |       |      |

## Answers to Quiz

1. North has a good hand, an opening bid or something near it, but does not know what game to bid. South's first choice should be three spades, if he has that suit, and his second, three no-trump if he has a heart stopper.
2. Again North wants to be in game but does not know where. He probably has a hand on which he would have used Stayman. South should show a spade suit if he has one.
3. This is the exceptional case in which the bid of the opponent's suit is natural. If North had a strong hand he would have bid the first time. He presumably has a long strong spade suit and not much else. South should pass with almost any hand.
4. North is not sure what game to bid. He probably has a moderate hand with some length in both major suits, and South should select a major.
5. This is quite different. The partnership is committed to game or higher in hearts, so North is showing control and slam ambitions. South will sign off in four hearts if his hand is unsuitable for a slam. If it is suitable, he will cue-bid an ace in his turn or make some other positive move toward slam.

# 11

# The Gadgets

Standard American bidding is basically a *natural* system of bidding. Most players, however, tack on a few *artificial* conventions or "gadgets." For example, almost everyone plays Blackwood. Here, bids of four and five no-trump as well as all the responses are artificial bids. When the Blackwood player bids four no-trump, he's not using the bid in a natural sense. He doesn't want to play no-trump. Similarly, when his partner responds five hearts, he's not trying to play hearts. He's making an artificial response which shows he holds two aces.

Good pairs usually adopt several artificial devices. They choose the ones they feel are most useful, are easy to remember, and don't interfere seriously with the rest of their bidding.

There's a group of players, however, particularly among the younger generation, who appear to be addicted to artificial bidding. These "scientists," as they're called, tack onto their bidding system one new gadget after another until the Standard American structure underneath can hardly be recognized. Eventually, the cumulative weight of this Rube Goldberg contraption proves to be their undoing. Meanwhile, it's extremely irritating to opponents, because they're forced to learn what each of the gadgets means in order to defend against it properly.

If you are a new duplicate player just starting out in

the tournament world, you may be awed by the gadgets being used on all sides of you. You'll probably decide that if you're going to get anywhere in this jungle you'd better grab some gadgets for yourself. You may even jump to the erroneous conclusion that if one gadget is good, twenty gadgets must be twenty times as good. Forget it! The way to improve your bridge is to cut down on your mistakes. Twenty gadgets will get you nothing but a series of headaches.

So before you leap merrily into the scientific camp, remember that for each gadget you add, there are two penalties to pay. First, you must give up the natural meaning of the bid involved. Second, each gadget you adopt puts an additional tax on your memory and that of your partner. Human memory is not infallible. Three or four gadgets may be all right, but when you're carrying too many in your mind you're bound to forget one sometime in the heat of the battle. And the catastrophe that can occur when a convention is forgotten may easily outweigh all the benefits ever derived from it.

In the case of Blackwood, the penalties are very slight in comparison with the potential gain. For example, in the following auction

| SOUTH | NORTH |
|-------|-------|
| 1 ♡   | 3 ♡   |
| 4 NT  |       |

the four no-trump bid wouldn't have much use as a natural bid. Furthermore, it's such a "shocking" bid, it serves to jar the memory. Players are very unlikely to forget Blackwood.

In contrast, let's take a look at the popular Texas convention. Texas is a form of transfer bid over partner's opening no-trump. The idea is to make the no-trump bidder the declarer of the final contract so that the opening lead will come up to the strong hand. If partner opens one no-trump and you hold a long string of hearts, you bid four diamonds. Partner is required to bid four hearts. If you hold a long spade suit, you bid four hearts and partner must correct to four spades. The Texas convention works well on a hand such as

NORTH
♠ K Q J x x x x
♡ 10 x
◇ Q x
♣ x x

SOUTH
♠ A 10 x
♡ A Q J 9
◇ K x x
♣ K x x

If North-South were using the Texas convention the bidding would go

| SOUTH | NORTH |
|-------|-------|
| 1 NT | 4 ♡ |
| 4 ♠ | Pass |

Played by South, four spades can hardly fail. Without Texas, however, North would become declarer and the contract would be in jeopardy with a club lead from East.

Doesn't this sound convincing? It sold me. Begrudgingly I adopted Texas and used it in tournaments with different partners for two years. Let me tell you how I fared.

During this period, my partner or I used the gadget five times. On four of these hands we broke even because it turned out that it didn't matter who was on lead. On the fifth hand we got a top score. One good hand in two years! No, neither of us forgot the convention. But for two years I carried the nagging worry in the back of my mind that I might forget. Imagine the tragedy in the example above if South forgot and passed North's bid of four hearts!

It's hard enough to play good bridge without continually having to waste mental effort to remember a gadget that's going to bring you a good result so rarely. After two years, I decided the headache far exceeded the benefits and I gave Texas back to the Indians.

Whether or not you adopt any artificial gadgets, you should be familiar with the more common ones so you'll understand what your opponents are doing. Here's a brief description of some of the more valuable popular conventions used in the United States today.

## Blackwood

A bid of four no-trump, *except where it is a direct raise of partner's no-trump bid*, is conventional and asks partner to show how many aces he holds. The responses are as follows:

*With no aces or all four aces*, bid five clubs.

*With one ace*, bid five diamonds.

*With two aces,* bid five hearts.

*With three aces*, bid five spades.

At this point, *if all the aces are accounted for*, the Blackwood bidder may now bid five no-trump to ask for kings, and his partner answers as follows:

*With no kings or all four kings*, bid six clubs.

*With one king*, bid six diamonds.

*With two kings*, bid six hearts.

*With three kings*, bid six spades.

I am sometimes asked how is partner to tell whether you have no aces or all four aces when you bid five clubs? This reminds me of the story of the two biology majors.

First student: "What's the difference between an elephant and a butterfly?"

Second student: "I don't know."

First student: "So, maybe you should major in something else?"

If partner can't tell from the bidding whether you have no aces or all four aces, he should give up bridge and try something else.

Most players overwork the Blackwood convention. In general, Blackwood should *not* be used as a means of getting to a slam. Before you use Blackwood you should already know that the partnership has sufficient values to make a slam. Blackwood should be used as a means of *staying out of a slam* in case two aces are missing. Keep this in mind also. When the Blackwood bidder says five no-trump, he's not just asking about kings for his own amusement. The five no-trump bid guarantees all the aces and indicates interest in a grand slam.

Don't use Blackwood unless you know what you're going to do after partner responds. A player with a void, for example, should rarely use Blackwood because he may not know what to do next.

If responder has a void, he may show it if he thinks it will prove useful to partner. (A void in an opponent's suit is probably useful. A void in partner's suit is better ignored.) The accepted way to show a void is to give the correct Blackwood response, but at the six level instead of the five level. Thus, over partner's bid of four no-trump, with two aces and a *useful* void, respond six hearts instead of five hearts.

When the Blackwood bidder finds out that he is missing two aces he will occasionally wish to play the hand in five no-trump. Naturally he cannot bid five no-trump himself because partner will think he is asking for kings. The standard way to sign off at five no-trump is for the Blackwood bidder to bid five of some suit other than the agreed trump suit. This requests responder to bid five no-trump.

Example:

| | SOUTH | | NORTH |
|---|---|---|---|
| ♠ | K Q 10 | ♠ | J 2 |
| ♡ | A K J | ♡ | Q 10 3 |
| ◇ | J | ◇ | K Q 4 |
| ♣ | K J 8 6 3 2 | ♣ | A Q 10 5 4 |

The bidding:

| SOUTH | NORTH |
|-------|-------|
| 1 ♣ | 3 ♣ |
| 4 NT | 5 ◇ |
| 5 ♡ | 5 NT |
| Pass | |

## The Stayman Convention

As a general rule, when you and partner together hold eight or more cards in a major suit, it's easier to make game in that suit than in no-trump. The ruffing power is usually worth a trick or two. Furthermore the fact that you have a fit in one suit increases the chances that another suit will be inadequately stopped at no-trump.

When your partner opens one no-trump and you hold a game-going hand with five or more cards in a major suit, it's a simple matter to locate an eight-card fit. (See the sections on responses to one no-trump, Chapter 3.) However, if the eight cards are divided four-four between the two hands, it's not so easy to discover the fit after an opening bid of one no-trump.

Example:

| WEST | EAST |
|------|------|
| ♠ K J x | ♠ Q 10 x x |
| ♡ K 10 9 x | ♡ Q J x x |
| ◇ A x | ◇ 10 x x |
| ♣ A J x x | ♣ K Q |

Using natural methods the bidding would go:

| WEST | EAST |
|------|------|
| 1 NT | 3 NT |

With a diamond lead there's almost no play for three no-trump despite the 26 high-card points. Yet four hearts is an excellent contract. How can you get to four hearts on these cards?

The Stayman convention is a device specifically designed to locate the four-four major suit fit after an opening bid of one no-trump. Here's the procedure. When partner opens one no-trump, if you're interested in learning whether he holds a four-card major suit you bid two clubs. (This is an artificial bid and has nothing to do with clubs.) Partner responds as follows:

*With four spades,* he bids two spades.
*With four hearts*, he bids two hearts.
*With no four-card major*, he bids two diamonds.

The Stayman bidder should now be in a good position to locate the best final contract.

Example 1.

| WEST | EAST |
|------|------|
| ♠ A Q 10 x | ♠ K J x x |
| ♡ K Q x | ♡ J 10 x x |
| ◊ K 10 x x | ◊ A Q |
| ♣ Q 10 | ♣ x x x |

Playing Stayman, the bidding would go

| WEST | EAST |
|------|------|
| 1 NT | 2 ♣ |
| 2 ♠ | 4 ♠ |

Notice that four spades is an excellent contract, whereas three no-trump is a very poor one.

Example 2.

| WEST | EAST |
|------|------|
| ♠ Q 10 | ♠ K J x x |
| ♡ K Q x | ♡ J 10 x x |
| ◊ K 10 x x | ◊ A Q |
| ♣ A Q 10 x | ♣ x x x |

| WEST | EAST |
|------|------|
| 1 NT | 2 ♣ |
| 2 ◊ | 3 NT |

Here, all the cards are the same as in Example 1 except that West's holdings in the black suits have been reversed. Once East discovers that no fit exists in the major suits, he bids three no-trump, confident that the partnership total of 27 points will afford an excellent play for the contract.

Example 3.

| WEST | EAST |
|------|------|
| ♠ K x | ♠ A 10 x x |
| ♡ A x x | ♡ K x x x |
| ◇ A x x x | ◇ J x |
| ♣ K Q 10 x | ♣ J x x |

| WEST | EAST |
|------|------|
| 1 NT | 2 ♣ |
| 2 ◇ | 2 NT |
| Pass | |

In this case East has about the equivalent of an immediate raise to two no-trump. He first uses Stayman in an effort to locate a four-four major suit fit. When this fails he bids two no-trump. West passes because his original bid was a minimum.

Example 4.

| WEST | EAST |
|------|------|
| ♠ A K x x | ♠ x x |
| ♡ K 10 x x | ♡ A Q x x |
| ◇ Q J | ◇ K x |
| ♣ K J 10 | ♣ Q x x x x |

| WEST | EAST |
|------|------|
| 1 NT | 2 ♣ |
| 2 ♠ | 3 NT |
| 4 ♡ | Pass |

In this hand, West has two four-card majors. Which should he bid first? If he has no agreement with partner on the subject, I recommend bidding the better suit first.

When East jumps to three no-trump, West reasons that his partner must have had some purpose in using Stayman so he corrects to four hearts. Notice that four hearts is an excellent contract, whereas three no-trump will fail with a diamond lead.

When you play Stayman, there is of course no way to stop in a contract of two clubs after partner has opened with one no-trump. This isn't a serious drawback, however, because if two clubs is all you can make the opponents will scarcely let you play it there. On the occasional hand where you wish to play in a club partial after partner has opened one no-trump, you may bid two clubs and rebid three clubs over partner's next bid.

Example 5.

| WEST | EAST |
|------|------|
| 1 NT | 2 ♣ |
| 2 ♡ | 3 ♣ |
| Pass | |

East's bid of three clubs is a sign-off and West is expected to pass.

Some players like to play a direct bid of three clubs in response to one no-trump as the weak bid with a long club suit. In this case they would play the sequence in Example 5 as a slam try in clubs.

This is a matter of choice, and before playing with a new partner it is important to discuss the meaning of both sequences.

Stayman may occasionally be used by a very weak hand that is short in clubs.

Example 6.
Partner opens one no-trump and you hold   ♠ J x x x ♡ x x x x ◇ J x x x x ♣ —. Bid two clubs and pass partner's response whether it's two diamonds, two hearts, or two spades.

## Two-Way Stayman

Many tournament players now use "Two-Way Stayman," an extension of the basic convention giving it two levels. A response of two diamonds to one no-trump asks similarly about major suits but also guarantees a game. In view of this, the opener can safely rebid at the level of three to show a five-card suit.

| WEST | EAST |
|------|------|
| 1 NT | 2 ◊ |
| 3 ♣ | |

West has a five-card club suit, a crumb of information that may help East to select the best game or judge slam prospects.

As in the normal version, the opener bids a major if he can.

| WEST | EAST |
|------|------|
| 1 NT | 2 ◊ |
| 2 ♡ | |

East is still captain, and if he now jumps to game in hearts, no-trump, or even some other strain, the bidding is over. If he is undecided about the right final contract, he can bid slowly. A new suit would promise at least five cards. Two no-trump would simply mark time and ask West to show another suit. And a raise to three hearts would be a clear slam invitation.

If West has neither a five-card suit nor a major, he simply responds two no-trump to the two-diamond enquiry.

The two-way procedure simplifies the problem of responding with minor-suit hands.

| WEST | EAST |
|------|------|
| 1 NT | 3 ♣ or 3 ◊ |

Both these bids show weak hands with six-card or longer suits. East is not interested in game, and West must pass.

With a moderate hand on which game is possible but not certain East would start with two clubs. And with a stronger hand he still would start with two diamonds.

If the responder bids a major at his second turn the precise meaning depends on the type of Stayman in use. Consider these two sequences.

| WEST | EAST |  | WEST | EAST |
|------|------|--|------|------|
| 1 NT | 2 ♣ |  | 1 NT | 2 ♣ |
| 2 ♦ | 2 ♠ |  | 2 ♦ | 3 ♠ |
| (a) |  |  | (b) |  |

Playing traditional one-way Stayman sequence (a) is invitational, showing about 8 points, and sequence (b) is forcing.

But using two-way Stayman, sequence (a) is discouraging and sequence (b) is invitational.

In all cases the responder shows at least a five-card suit.

Over an opening bid of two no-trump, three clubs is Stayman. With a four-card major, partner rebids three hearts or three spades. With no four-card major he rebids three diamonds.

Example:

| WEST | EAST |
|------|------|
| ♠ A Q x x | ♠ J 10 x x |
| ♡ A 10 x | ♡ Q J x x |
| ♦ A K J | ♦ Q x x |
| ♣ A 10 x | ♣ x x |

Using Stayman, the bidding would go

| WEST | EAST |
|------|------|
| 2 NT | 3 ♣ |
| 3 ♠ | 4 ♠ |

Notice that three no-trump is in jeopardy with a club lead, while four spades is virtually foolproof.

Valuable though it is, Stayman has one serious drawback. Like alcohol, it gets in the user's bloodstream and he can't leave it alone. When partner opens one no-trump, many players feel a tremendous urge to bid two clubs almost without sorting their cards. Unfortunately, the poor results achieved by using Stayman when it shouldn't be used more than overcome the profits from using it properly.

In conclusion, the Stayman convention is a valuable tool for locating a four-card major suit in the no-trump bidder's hand. However, like most conventions it is overworked and should be used only when necessary.

## The Gerber Convention

Gerber, like Blackwood, is a convention designed to find out how many aces partner holds. Unlike Blackwood, however, Gerber is primarily useful in no-trump auctions.

If partner opens one no-trump and you hold a hand such as ♠ x ♡ K Q J x x x x x ◊ K Q 10 ♣ x, your only concern is the number of aces in partner's hand. If he holds three aces, you want to play six hearts. If he holds four aces you want to play seven no-trump. You can't use Blackwood at this point, however, because a bid of four no-trump when it's a direct raise of partner's no-trump bid is not Blackwood at all but rather a quantitative raise of no-trump. The simplest solution is to employ the Gerber four-club convention.

Over one no-trump, a jump to four clubs is an artificial bid and asks for aces. Partner responds as follows:

*With no aces or four aces,* he bids four diamonds.
*With one ace,* he bids four hearts.
*With two aces,* he bids four spades.
*With three aces,* he bids four no-trump.

If all the aces are accounted for and the Gerber bidder is interested in a grand slam, he may now bid five clubs to inquire about kings. Partner responds as follows:

*With no king or four kings*, he bids five diamonds.

*With one king*, he bids five hearts.

*With two kings*, he bids five spades.

*With three kings*, he bids five no-trump.

Most good players use a jump to four clubs directly over an opening bid of one or two no-trump as Gerber. Some also play four clubs as Gerber in other sequences. There's always the danger, however, that in other sequences there'll be a conflict between Gerber and the natural meaning of four clubs. To avoid confusion I recommend playing four clubs as Gerber *only* over opening bids of one, two, and possibly three no-trump. Some people play four clubs over an opening bid of three no-trump as Stayman and some play it as Gerber. So, if you haven't discussed it with partner, you should avoid the bid.


### The Weak Two-Bid

Today, most tournament players in the United States play an opening bid of two spades, two hearts, and two diamonds as weak bids. A typical weak two-bid may look like ♠ K Q J x x x ♡ x x ◇ K 10 x ♣ x x.

Playing weak two-bids, you'd open this hand with a bid of two spades. The chief advantage of the bid is that your opponents may have trouble finding their best contract after your pre-emptive opening. Your partner, on the other hand, should find it relatively easy to determine the best spot for your side because he's already received a clear picture of your hand. He knows (1) you don't have enough to open with a one-bid, and (2) you have a six-card suit and about a trick and a half in high cards with most of your strength concentrated in the long suit. Note: A weak two-bid denies holding a four-card major suit on the side.

## Responses to Weak Two-Bids

Most people play that any bid other than a raise is forcing over the weak two-bid. A raise is usually played as a continuation of the pre-empt.

Example 1.

| WEST | EAST |
|------|------|
| 2 ♡  | 2 ♠  |

West must bid again. With a minimum he rebids three hearts. With a maximum he makes some other bid depending on his hand.

Example 2.

| WEST | EAST |
|------|------|
| 2 ♡  | 3 ♡  |

West must pass. East doesn't have a good hand. He's simply trying to make life difficult for the enemy.

Example 3.

| WEST | EAST |
|------|------|
| 2 ♡  | 2 NT |

This response is artificial and asks West to describe his hand further.

If West holds a minimum he will rebid his suit. He would therefore bid three hearts holding ♠ x x ♡ K Q 10 9 x x ◇ x x x ♣ x x.

If West has a better hand he will bid a side-suit in which he has a "feature," usually an ace or a king. Three diamonds would be the bid with this hand ♠ x x ♡ K Q 10 9 x x ◇ K J x ♣ x x.

And if West's suit is solid he bids three no-trump. This would be his choice with ♠ x x ♡ A K Q 10 x x ◇ x x x ♣ x x. East may then decide to play for nine tricks and pass.

Note: Some players play that two no-trump is the only forcing response to the weak two-bid. In that case a new suit bid is a sign-off. It is important to discuss with your partner whether or not new suit responses are forcing.

## Defense to the Weak Two-Bid

When your opponent opens with a weak two-bid, the best defense is to treat it like a one-bid. In the following examples your right-hand opponent deals and makes a weak bid of two hearts:

Example 1.
You hold ♠ A K J x x x ♡ x x ◇ A J x ♣ J x.
Bid two spades.

Example 2.
You hold ♠ A J 10 x ♡ x x ◇ A J 9 x ◇ K Q x.
Double for a take-out. You have a good opening bid and support for any suit your partner may choose.

Example 3.
You hold ♠ A 10 x ♡ A Q x ◇ K J x x ♣ K J x.
Bid two no-trump. This shows a balanced hand, usually a double heart stopper, and at least the high-card equivalent of an opening one no-trump bid.

Example 4.
You hold ♠ A 10 ♡ A Q 10 9 x ◇ x x x x ♣ K x.
Pass. You can't double for penalties because a double of any low-level contract *when partner has never bid* is for take-out. If you double, partner will act on the assumption that you have something like Example 2, and you may end up in the soup. Your best bet is to pass and take a small profit. Of course, if your partner should double you can leave it in.

## The Artificial Two-Club Opening

When two spades, two hearts, and two diamonds are used as weak bids, the bid of two clubs is reserved for the strong hand *regardless of suit*.

Example:

| | WEST | | EAST |
|---|---|---|---|
| ♠ | A K J 10 x x x | ♠ | x x x |
| ♡ | A K x | ♡ | Q x |
| ◇ | x | ◇ | Q x x |
| ♣ | A x | ♣ | x x x x x |

Playing strong two-bids, the bidding on this hand might go as follows:

| WEST | EAST |
|---|---|
| 2 ♠ | 2 NT |
| 3 ♠ | 4 ♠ |

Playing weak two-bids, the bidding would go:

| WEST | EAST |
|---|---|
| 2 ♣ | 2 ◇ |
| 2 ♠ | 2 NT |
| 3 ♠ | 4 ♠ |

Here, two clubs announces a game-going hand but doesn't specify the suit. West's next bid will identify the suit. East's bid of two diamonds is negative. Just as two no-trump is the negative response to a strong two-bid, two diamonds is the negative response to an artificial two-club bid. Thereafter the bidding is natural.

Players who use weak two-bids also open two clubs with a balanced hand containing 23 or 24 points and rebid two no-trump over partner's response. Thus they are able to play that an opening bid of two no-trump is limited to 21 or 22 points.

## The Grand Slam Force

Occasionally you get a hand where a small slam is assured and the only thing keeping you from bidding a grand slam is the fear of a trump loser. The grand slam force of five no-trump is designed for this type of hand, where your only concern is the ace, king, or queen of trumps.

Example:

| | WEST | EAST |
|---|---|---|
| ♠ | A Q x | ♠ K J x x x |
| ♡ | J x x | ♡ A K Q x x |
| ◇ | K Q x | ◇ A x x |
| ♣ | A J x x | ♣ — |

The bidding:

| WEST | EAST |
|---|---|
| 1 NT | 3 ♠ |
| 4 ♠ | 5 NT |
| 7 ♠ | |

When West opens the bidding with one no-trump, East knows immediately there's a slam in either spades or hearts. When West raises spades, East realizes there should be thirteen tricks in the hand if West has both the ace and queen of spades. A jump to five no-trump in this situation is an artificial bid and asks partner to bid seven in the agreed trump suit if he holds two of the three top honors. Holding the ace and queen of spades, West obediently bids the grand slam.

## The Landy Convention

When your right-hand opponent opens the bidding with one no-trump, it's sometimes difficult as well as dangerous to enter the auction. With 16 or more points you can double. With less than 16 points you can overcall if you have a powerful suit. But what about the hands where you have less than 16 points and no powerful suit?

There have been several conventions invented for use over an opponent's no-trump bid. The simplest of these is the Landy two-club bid. Playing Landy, a bid of two clubs over an opponent's no-trump is a take-out bid showing 15 points or less and good support for both major suits.

Example:
Your right-hand opponent opens one no-trump. You hold
♠ A Q x x x   ♡ K J 10 x   ◇ x x   ♣ K x.   Playing Landy you bid two clubs. Partner is requested to bid his better major.

Without Landy it would be dangerous to enter the auction with this hand. If you double, partner will play you for 16 or more points. If he holds 5 points, he'll assume your side has more than half the high-card strength and will pass expecting to beat one no-trump doubled (and possibly redoubled). This could be fatal. On the other hand, to overcall two hearts or two spades on this hand would be lunacy. If you pick the wrong suit, you may well be carried out on a stretcher. Without Landy, then, you have to pass even though the hand could belong to your side in a heart or spade partial.

Playing Landy you can act with relative safety. By allowing partner to pick his longer major you have almost eliminated the danger of playing in the wrong suit. If partner has no four-card major, he bids a three-card major. And if he has no three-card major, he must have a long minor suit. In this case he can pass two clubs or escape to two diamonds.

Landy may also be used in the fourth position.

Example:

| WEST | NORTH | EAST | SOUTH |
|------|-------|------|-------|
| 1 NT | Pass  | Pass | 2 ♣   |

It's somewhat easier for South to compete in this position because East is now known to have at most about seven points. Therefore, North is marked with some strength. A double or an overcall or a Landy take-out of two clubs may be made on about a king less in fourth position than in second position.

Of course, if you play Landy you can't overcall one no-trump with two clubs when you hold a genuine club suit.

Example:
Right-hand opponent opens one no-trump. You hold ♠ K J 10  ♡ x x  ◇ x x.  ♣ A Q J 10 x x. If you're not using the Landy convention you'd overcall two clubs. Playing Landy you must pass. (With one more club you might risk an overcall of three clubs.) The point is that you cannot bid two clubs naturally over one no-trump if you're playing Landy. However, this is not much of a sacrifice, because if you can make a club partial the opponents will surely be able to make a partial in a higher-ranking suit. They'll be able to outbid you. When you play Landy you give up the club suit in exchange for the more important spade or heart fit.

The greatest danger in playing Landy is that you or your partner will forget it. Landy is not recommended for casual partnerships.

### The Unusual No-Trump

Sometimes it's impossible for a no-trump bid to have its normal meaning.

Example 1.

| WEST | NORTH | EAST | SOUTH |
|------|-------|------|-------|
| 1 NT | 2 NT  | Pass | ?     |

Here, North has overcalled the opponent's bid of one no-trump with a bid of two no-trump. Obviously this is an unusual bid. North cannot have a strong no-trump hand or he would double. Common sense tells us that North doesn't want to play no-trump at all but actually has a very distributional hand. He can't have a one-suited hand or he would have bid his suit. The answer is he has a two-suited hand and wants his partner to choose between

138

the two suits. In the United States, the unusual no-trump has long been associated specifically with the two minor suits. On the bidding given above, North may hold ♠ x ♡ x ◇ K Q 10 9 x x ♣ A Q J 10 x. His bid of two no-trump over opponent's one no-trump is the unusual no-trump and asks South to bid his longer minor.

Similarly, the bidding might go as follows:

Example 2.

| WEST | NORTH | EAST | SOUTH |
|------|-------|------|-------|
| 1 ♡ | Pass | 1 NT | 2 NT |

South can't have a strong no-trump type of hand or he would double. Here, South has used the unusual no-trump and is asking North to bid his longer minor.

The unusual no-trump has been extended to apply in the following cases:

Example 3.

| WEST | NORTH | | WEST | NORTH |
|------|-------|-----|------|-------|
| 1 ♠ | 2 NT | or | 1 ♡ | 2 NT |

The reasoning here is that it would be quite unlikely for North to hold a standard two no-trump bid after West has opened the bidding. If he did hold a standard two no-trump, he could always double and bid two no-trump on the next round. The jump to two no-trump after an opening bid by the opponent of one spade or one heart is therefore reserved for a distributional freak in the minors.

A jump bid of two no-trump after an opening bid by an opponent of one diamond or one club is used by some players to show a distributional freak *in the two cheaper unbid suits*.

Example 4.

| WEST | NORTH |
|------|-------|
| 1 ◇ | 2 NT |

North has hearts and clubs,

and

| | WEST | NORTH |
|---|---|---|
| | 1 ♣ | 2 NT |

North has hearts and diamonds.

The sequences in Examples 3 and 4 should never be used unless they have been discussed specifically with partner beforehand.

The sequences given in Examples 1, 2, 3, and 4 all occur very rarely because one seldom holds sufficient length and strength in both minors to safely force partner to make a bid at the three level in the middle of an active auction by the enemy. Remember, partner may have to bid on a two-card suit! When the bidding has died, however, the unusual no-trump may be used more readily because the opponents have limited their strength and the danger is greatly reduced.

Example 5.

| WEST | NORTH | EAST | SOUTH |
|---|---|---|---|
| 1 ♠ | Pass | 2 ♠ | Pass |
| Pass | ? | | |

What should North bid if he holds ♠ x x ♡ x ◊ K J 10 x x ♣ A J 10 x x? Although he could not safely take any action over one spade with such a weak hand, he should reconsider now that the bidding has died. In the first place, South is now marked with some strength. There are 40 points in the deck. North has 9 points, so the other three players have 31. East-West have made no effort to get to game despite their spade fit, so they have considerably less than 26 points between them. On this auction, South figures to hold about 9 to 12 points. In the second place, the fact that East-West have a fit increases the chances that North-South also have a fit. Why sell out for two spades when North-South can probably take nine tricks in a minor-suit contract?

A double by North at this point would ask South to bid

his best suit. Obviously North can't double because South might choose hearts. The proper bid by North is two no-trump (the unusual no-trump), which asks South to bid his longer minor suit.

An immediate one no-trump overcall shows 16 to 18 points, a balanced hand, and usually a double stopper in opponent's suit. Thus, if the bidding goes

| WEST | NORTH |
|------|-------|
| 1 ♠ | 1 NT |

North must hold something like ♠ A Q x ♡ K x x ◊ A J 9 x ♣ Q J x. Don't confuse this immediate overcall of one no-trump with the unusual no-trump. There's nothing unusual about it.

The following case is unusual, however:

Example 6.

| NORTH | EAST | SOUTH | WEST |
|-------|------|-------|------|
| Pass | Pass | Pass | 1 ♠ |
| 1 NT | | | |

Here, North can't possibly hold the requirements for a standard overcall of one no-trump because he is a passed hand. It's much too dangerous to overcall one no-trump on a balanced hand that's not even worth an opening bid. Thus, an overcall of one no-trump *by a passed hand* is "unusual" and asks partner to choose a minor.

When two suits have been bid, the unusual no-trump calls for the two unbid suits.

Example 7.

| WEST | NORTH | EAST | SOUTH |
|------|-------|------|-------|
| 1 ♠ | Pass | 2 ◊ | 2 NT |

South is showing length in clubs and hearts, the two unbid suits. This use of the unusual no-trump makes sense because it would be highly dangerous for South to stick his neck out between two bidding opponents with a balanced hand. (With a really good hand he could double.) His actual bid of two no-trump in this auction should look something like ♠ x ♡ K Q 10 9 x ◇ x x ♣ K Q J 10 x.

## Negative Doubles

If you play standard bridge without any conventions, the double of an overcall is for penalties.

| NORTH | EAST | SOUTH | WEST |
|-------|------|-------|------|
| 1 ♠ | 2 ◇ | Double | |

South probably holds something like:

Hand A: ♠ x x ♡ A K x ◇ K J 9 x ♣ x x x x

North is expected to pass, and poor East will be considerably out of pocket by the time the hand is over.

But the opportunity for such doubles comes rather rarely, and many tournament players change the meaning of such doubles from penalty to take-out. This becomes an exception to the general rule that doubles are for penalties whenever partner has bid.

Such doubles are called negative, and it is important to agree with partner the situations in which they will apply. Suppose that you have agreed to play "negative doubles through two spades." In the above sequence East's overcall is not above two spades and your double would be negative, i.e., take-out, promising at least four cards in hearts, the unbid major suit. The doubler would hold something like this:

Hand B: ♠ x x ♡ A K x x ◇ x x ♣ Q x x x x

Note that if you were not playing negative doubles you would have no sensible bid with Hand B. You cannot bid two hearts, which would show a five-card heart suit and at least 10 points. And you certainly are not strong enough to bid three clubs.

Playing negative doubles, however, Hand A will annoy you. Your best course would be to bid two no-trump, giving up the chance of a juicy penalty. A player with length in the enemy suit sometimes passes, hoping that his partner will reopen with a double which he will pass for penalties.

The crucial question is whether situation A or situation B arises more often. At the one-level the answer is clearly situation B, but it becomes less clear the higher you go.

You rarely get rich doubling anyone for penalties at the one-level. Therefore serious tournament players should make some use of the negative double. The basic situation, which many players regard as sufficient for their purpose, is this:

| NORTH | EAST | SOUTH |
|-------|------|-------|
| 1 ♣ or 1 ♢ | 1 ♠ | Double |

South shows at least four hearts and at least 6 points. Example: ♠ x x x  ♡ K x x x  ◇ A x x  ♣ x x x. The doubler will not bid again voluntarily—he has described his hand. Another example: ♠ x x x  ♡ A J x x x  ◇ J x  ♣ x x. This time the doubler will follow with two hearts if he has the chance, showing a long suit and a weak hand, not strong enough to bid two hearts originally.

This would apply also if the overcall was two spades instead of one spade, but the doubler would need to be slightly stronger, a minimum of 8 points.

For those using the wider spectrum of negative doubles here are some other sequences.

| NORTH | EAST | SOUTH |
|-------|------|-------|
| 1 ♣ | 1 ◇ | Double |

South promises 6 or more points and exactly four cards in each major suit. With other holdings he would bid a major himself.

| NORTH | EAST | SOUTH |
|-------|------|-------|
| 1 ♣ | 1 ♡ | Double |

South has exactly four spades and 6 or more points. With more spades he would bid the suit.

It is of course vital to agree on the level through which you play negative doubles. If you play them through three spades, as many experts do, you will thereby solve some tricky bidding problems but give up some lucrative penalty doubles. If you play them through five diamonds, as a few experts actually do, you are giving up almost all your ability to punish an incautious opponent.

It is important to remember that negative doubles promise 6 points at the one-level, 8 points at the two-level, and 10 points at the three-level. And, of course, they promise at least four cards in any unbid major.

Do not use a negative double when you have a natural bid available.

| NORTH | EAST | SOUTH |
|-------|------|-------|
| 1 ◊ | 1 ♠ | ? |

You hold ♠ x x  ♡ A Q J x x  ◊ A J x  ♣ x x x.

Bid two hearts. If you double, your partner will assume you had a reason for not bidding two hearts, either inadequate hearts or an inadequate hand. However:

♠ x x x  ♡ A K x x  ◊ A K x  ♣ x x x

Make a negative double, since a bid of two hearts would promise a five-card suit. However partner will not expect you to have so much strength so you will have to put him in game on the next round.

Warning: Negative doubles do not apply when no-trump is involved.

| NORTH | EAST | SOUTH | WEST |
|-------|------|-------|------|
| 1 ◇   | 1 NT | Double |     |

This is a penalty double. South knows that his side has the majority of the high-card points.

| NORTH | EAST | SOUTH | WEST |
|-------|------|-------|------|
| 1 NT  | 2 ◇  | Double |     |

Again this is a penalty double. South could have ♠ x x ♡ A K x ◇ Q 9 x x ♣ x x x x and East-West are in serious trouble.

### The Jacoby Transfer Bid

The Jacoby Transfer Bid is very much like the Texas convention discussed earlier, but the transfer operates at the two-level instead of the four-level. In response to one no-trump, two diamonds shows five or more hearts, and two hearts shows five or more spades.

In each of the following examples you have agreed to play Jacoby Transfers and partner opens one no-trump. What do you bid?

Example 1.
♠ x x  ♡ Q 9 x x x x  ◇ Q x x  ♣ x x

Bid two diamonds. Partner is now required to bid two hearts, and you will gladly pass. This makes him the declarer, a slight advantage since the opening lead will come up to his strong hand.

Example 2.
♠ x  ♡ K Q J x x x  ◇ Q J x x  ♣ x x

Bid two diamonds, and when partner bids two hearts bid four hearts.

Example 3.
♠ K J x x x  ♡ A x  ◇ x x x  ♣ x x x

Bid two hearts, and when partner bids two spades, you then bid two no-trump. He will know that you have exactly five spades, 8 or 9 points, and a balanced hand, probably with 5–3–3–2 distribution. With a slightly stronger hand, 10 points or more, you would bid three no-trump at your second turn.

Example 4.
♠ KJxxx ♡ x ♦ Axxxx ♣ Ax

Bid two hearts, showing five spades, and follow with three diamonds, a natural forcing bid. This will leave all doors open and allow partner to judge the extent to which the hands fit. The right final contract might be three no-trump, four or six spades, or five or six diamonds.

A response of two clubs is still the Stayman convention (*not* the two-way variety) and is generally used when the responder has a four-card major.

The response of two spades is usually used to show a good hand with length in both minors and slam interest. The opener bids a minor suit if he has one, establishing a fit, and otherwise bids two no-trump. Never use Jacoby Transfers without discussing the meaning of the two spade response.

Warning: Jacoby does not operate following interference.

| NORTH | EAST | SOUTH |
|-------|------|-------|
| 1 NT  | 2 ◊  | 2 ♡   |

South's bid of two hearts is not a transfer. He wants to play two hearts and North should pass.

| NORTH | EAST   | SOUTH |
|-------|--------|-------|
| 1 NT  | Double | 2 ◊   |

Again this is not a transfer. South has a bad hand and a long diamond suit. North must pass.

Summing up: While standard American bidding is basically *natural* bidding, most players tack on a few gadgets, or *artificial* bids, to help them meet special problems of bidding. In this chapter we've discussed several of the more common gadgets used in tournament play in the United States. You should be familiar with them so you'll know how to defend against them. There are dozens and dozens of others! Which ones you adopt, if any, is entirely up to you and your partner. But always keep in mind that for each *artificial* bid you superimpose on Standard American, you not only sacrifice a *natural* bid, but place an additional tax on the memories of yourself and your partner.

# 12

# The Opening Lead

In bridge, the defenders always get to fire the first shot. Just as the opening salvo can effect the result of a battle on the high seas, the opening lead can affect the result of a battle at the bridge table. The right lead can set the strategy of the defenders and make it difficult if not impossible for declarer to make his contract. The wrong lead, however, can hand it to him on a silver platter.

The problem of choosing a lead is twofold. First, you must decide which suit to lead. Second, you must decide which card in the suit.

Choosing the right suit is one of the toughest problems in the game of bridge and often stumps even the experts. Choosing the correct card within the suit, however, is practically automatic. Because it is so simple, we'll discuss it first.

Once you've decided to lead a certain suit, which card should you select? If you hold only one card in the suit there's no problem.

In the following examples, the underscored card is the correct lead.

*With two cards* in a suit, it is correct to lead the higher.

Example:  A̲ K  A̲ 2  K̲ 3  J̲ 5  7̲ 4

*With three small cards*, it is standard to lead the top card. (A nine or any lower card is considered "small" for this purpose.) However, some players agree to lead the bottom card, while others the middle card to be followed by the top. This point should be discussed with a new partner.

Example:  9 6 2   8 7 4   6 4 2

*With three to an honor*, it is correct to lead low, except that against a suit contract it is dangerous to lead away from an ace.

Example:
Against no-trump, lead   A 6 3   K 7 2   J 5 4   10 5 2.

Against a suit contract, lead   A 6 3   K 7 2   J 5 4   10 5 2.

*With any three-card holding headed by two touching cards*, it is correct to lead the top card, except that in the United States it is customary to lead the king from any combination that includes the ace and the king.

Example:  A K 5   K Q 2   Q J 6   J 10 7   10 9 4

*With four or more cards*, it is standard to lead the fourth best unless the suit is headed by a sequence, in which case it is correct to lead the top of the sequence.

Example:  Q 6 4 2   Q J 10 2

*Against a no-trump contract*, a sequence needs at least three cards. (K Q 10,  Q J 9,  J 10 8,  10 9 7 are also considered to be sequences.)

Example:  Against no-trump, lead  K Q J 4   Q J 9 2
Q J 6 2   A Q 6 3 2   8 6 4 2   J 7 5 4 3 2.

*Against a suit contract*, a sequence need only be two cards long. (Remember also that it is too dangerous to lead away from an ace against a suit contract.)

Example: Against a suit contract, lead A 8 6 4 2 K Q 6 2
Q J 5 3 8 6 4 2 Q 10 6 4 2.

## Returning the Suit Led by Partner

Many players don't realize that when *returning* a suit
it is correct to lead the *higher* card unless you held four
or more of the suit *originally*. In that case it is correct to
return the card *which originally was your fourth best*.

Example: Against a no-trump contract, West opens the
club five, and the suit is divided as follows:

DUMMY
♣ 6

WEST  EAST
♣ K J 9 5 3  ♣ A 8 4 2

DECLARER
♣ Q 10 7

East wins the first trick with the ace and should return
the two (the card which originally was his fourth best).
West is now able to count declarer's hand, and he cashes
the entire club suit.

If the clubs had been divided like this:

DUMMY
♣ 6

WEST  EAST
♣ K J 9 5 3  ♣ A 8 2

DECLARER
♣ Q 10 7 4

then East would win the first trick with the ace and return
the eight. South would cover with the ten and West would
win with the jack. This time, however, West knows he
cannot cash the entire suit immediately because declarer

still has the queen and one other club in his hand. So West exits with something else and sits back to wait for East to get in and lead his last club.

## Leading the Suit Partner Bid

There is a popular misconception that one should always lead the top of partner's suit. This is incorrect. When you lead partner's suit, you should select the correct card according to the rules above.

Example:

                    NORTH
                    ♠ K Q 6 2
                    ♡ A K 9 5 3
                    ◇ 5 3 2
                    ♣ 3

    WEST                        EAST
    ♠ 7 4                       ♠ 8
    ♡ J 4 2                     ♡ Q 10 8 7
    ◇ K 8 4                     ◇ A J 10 9
    ♣ J 9 7 5 4                 ♣ A Q 6 2

                    SOUTH
                    ♠ A J 10 9 5 3
                    ♡ 6
                    ◇ Q 7 6
                    ♣ K 10 8

The bidding:

| EAST | SOUTH | WEST | NORTH |
|------|-------|------|-------|
| 1 ◇ | 1 ♠ | Pass | 4 ♠ |
| Pass | Pass | Pass | |

Against the final contract of four spades, West wisely decides to lead his partner's suit. Holding three to an honor he correctly leads the four. East wins with the ace and returns the jack, trapping declarers' queen. The defense makes three diamond tricks and the club ace to set the

151

contract. If West had followed the old wives' tale and led the top of his partner's suit, declarer would have won the third trick with the queen and made his contract.

If you are not certain of what card to lead from any given holding, try the following short quiz.

## QUIZ ON WHICH CARD TO LEAD

*Against a no-trump contract*, which card do you lead from each of these holdings?

| | | | |
|---|---|---|---|
| 1. | 10 6 2 | 6. | A K 3 |
| 2. | A K 6 4 2 | 7. | Q J 10 4 |
| 3. | Q J 7 5 3 2 | 8. | Q J 9 8 |
| 4. | J 6 | 9. | K Q 3 2 |
| 5. | 8 6 3 2 | 10. | A 6 3 2 |

*Against a suit contract*, which card do you lead from each of these holdings?

| | | | |
|---|---|---|---|
| 11. | A 6 3 2 | 14. | A K 6 3 |
| 12. | 7 5 4 | 15. | K 4 |
| 13. | K Q 6 2 | | |

**Answers to Quiz**

| | | | |
|---|---|---|---|
| 1. | 2 | 9. | 2 |
| 2. | 4 | 10. | 2 |
| 3. | 5 | 11. | A |
| 4. | J | 12. | 7 |
| 5. | 2 | 13. | K |
| 6. | K | 14. | K |
| 7. | Q | 15. | K |
| 8. | Q | | |

# The Rule of Eleven

(The Corollary to the Conventional Lead of Fourth Best)

When partner leads his fourth-best card, you should immediately be able to tell how many cards declarer holds in his hand that are higher than the card partner led. A simple mechanical way to calculate this is called the rule of eleven.

Suppose partner leads the five. Subtract five from eleven and this will tell you how many cards higher than the five are held by dummy, you, and declarer, together. Now subtract those in dummy and your own hand and you have the number in declarer's hand.

Although every beginner learns this rule the average player tends to forget it in the heat of battle. For example:

```
                    NORTH
                 ♠ K 3
                 ♡ A K 9 5
                 ◇ A Q
                 ♣ K J 10 9 8

   WEST                         EAST
♠ Q 10 8 7 4                 ♠ A J 9 2
♡ 8                          ♡ 3
◇ J 7 6 2                    ◇ K 10 9 8 4
♣ Q 6 2                      ♣ A 7 4

                    SOUTH
                 ♠ 6 5
                 ♡ Q J 10 7 6 4 2
                 ◇ 3 5
                 ♣ 5 3
```

The bidding:

| EAST | SOUTH | WEST | NORTH |
|------|-------|------|-------|
| 1 ◇ | Pass | 1 ♠ | Double |
| 2 ♠ | 3 ♡ | Pass | 4 ♡ |
| Pass | Pass | Pass | |

Against the four-heart contract, West leads the spade seven (his fourth best) and dummy plays the three. The average East promptly wins with the jack and cashes the spade ace. He then starts to look around for a way to get into partner's hand for a diamond lead through dummy's ace-queen before declarer gets the clubs established. There is no way to get there, however, and declarer easily makes his game.

When West led the spade seven, East should have automatically said to himself, "Seven from eleven is four. Dummy and I together have four cards higher than the seven. Therefore declarer has none." East can therefore play the spade two on the first trick allowing West to hold the lead. West will switch to a diamond and declarer can no longer make the contract.

Now we get to the difficult matter of selecting the best suit to lead.

Many texts for beginners give a list of leads in the order of their desirability, with Rock of Gibraltar suggestions like king-queen-jack near the top of the list, and hideous combinations like ace-queen-small at the bottom. All other things being equal, one naturally should choose a suit where there is the safety of a solid sequence. But rarely in bridge are all other things equal. Before leading, it is important to consider carefully everything you know about declarer's hand, dummy's hand, and partner's hand as well as the thirteen cards you actually see. The success or failure of many a contract depends on the suit led. Unfortunately there is no table of leads nor a set of rules which can cover every situation. Good judgment is essential, and one way to develop good judgment is to study the following suggestions.

### Passive Defense versus Active Defense

There are two basic forms of defense: passive and active. In passive defense, the prime object of the defenders is to play safe. They concentrate on giving nothing away by their leads and they sit back to wait for those tricks which are rightfully theirs. In active defense, the defenders make aggressive and relatively dangerous leads in order to develop tricks which they might not otherwise get.

Hands which you expect to set generally call for passive or safe leads.

Example:

| SOUTH | WEST | NORTH | EAST |
|-------|------|-------|------|
| 1 ♠ | Pass | 2 ♠ | Pass |
| 3 ♠ | Pass | 4 ♠ | Pass |

As West you hold ♠ Q J 9 5 ♡ K 4 3 ◇ 10 9 8 4 3 ♣ 8. What do you lead? Answer: the diamond ten. You should expect to set this hand. From the bidding it is clear that North-South have no extra strength in reserve. They've reached a borderline contract, which they may make if everything goes well for them. You know, however, that declarer is in for a nasty shock in the trump suit. The bad trump break will surely spell defeat for this close game, and you shouldn't take any unnecessary risks in leading. A heart lead might jeopardize your king, while a club lead might sacrifice one of your partner's tricks. The best lead in this case is the passive lead of the diamond ten.

Hands in which declarer will probably make his contract call for aggressive or attacking leads.

Example:

| SOUTH | WEST | NORTH | EAST |
|-------|------|-------|------|
| 1 ♡ | Pass | 3 ◇ | Pass |
| 3 ♡ | Pass | 4 ♡ | Pass |
| 4 NT | Pass | 5 ♡ | Pass |
| 6 ♡ | Pass | Pass | Pass |

As West you hold ♠ J 10 9 8 7 ♡ 10 6 4 ◇ A 6 ♣ K 6 3. What do you lead? Answer: the club three. This bidding sounds quite confident, and it doesn't take too much imagination to visualize that dummy will look something like this:

DUMMY
♠ x
♡ A J x
◊ K Q J 10 x x
♣ A x x

YOU
♠ J 10 9 8 7
♡ 10 6 4
◊ A 6
♣ K 6 3

If you make the safe lead of the spade jack, declarer will make at least five heart tricks, five diamond tricks, and the two black aces for an easy slam. If, however, you make the risky and aggressive lead of a small club, and declarer has the club queen, you've lost nothing because you had nothing to lose. But if your partner should hold the club queen, you've struck gold!

"But," says the doubting Thomas, "How do I know dummy won't look like this instead?"

DUMMY
♠ A x x
♡ Q J x
◊ K Q J 10 x x
♣ A

Yes, dummy could look like that, but it's less likely, as you can tell from your own distribution in the black suits. The main point, however, is that if you play for this dummy, your partner must hold the spade *king* to set the contract. In view of the bidding, it's much more reasonable to hope partner has a side *queen* rather than a side *king*. The more modest your prayer, the better the chances of its being fulfilled.

## Leading Against No-Trump

Let's assume the opponents have bid three no-trump. To set them, you and your partner need five tricks. Before leading, consider where those five tricks are likely to come from.

Example:

| SOUTH | WEST | NORTH | EAST |
|-------|------|-------|------|
| 1 NT  | Pass | 3 NT  | Pass |
| Pass  | Pass |       |      |

As West you hold ♠ Q J 10　♡ A Q 7 4 3　◊ 6 4 ♣ 9 7 2. What do you lead? Answer: the heart four. The best way to develop the five tricks needed to defeat the contract is to attack the heart suit. Of course you are likely to sacrifice a heart trick on this lead, because declarer may well hold something like king-jack-small of hearts. But when your partner gets the lead he'll return a heart and you'll get four heart tricks for the one you lost. If you make the passive lead of the spade queen, the enemy, who have at least 26 points between them, will surely develop nine tricks before you get your five.

*Against a contract of three no-trump, or against a no-trump partial, it's usually wise to attack your longest and strongest suit.*

Occasionally it's better to attack your partner's suit than your own.

Example:

| SOUTH | WEST | NORTH | EAST |
|-------|------|-------|------|
| 1 NT  | Pass | 3 NT  | Pass |
| Pass  | Pass |       |      |

As West you hold ♠ 8 6 5 4 3 2　♡ J 10　◊ J 10 ♣ 9 7 2. What do you lead? Answer: the heart jack. In this situation it is pretty futile to attack spades. Even if you succeed in setting them up you have no entry to cash them. Partner has all the entries on this hand so it's better to set up *his* long suit. He is somewhat more likely to hold a major than a minor suit, because the enemy is more apt to conceal a minor suit in the bidding than a major.

## When Should You Lead Trumps?

A trump lead is effective when declarer can be expected to ruff losers in the dummy. When declarer has a two-suited hand it's very often right to lead trumps.

Example:

| SOUTH | WEST | NORTH | EAST |
|-------|------|-------|------|
| 1 ♠ | Pass | 2 ◊ | Pass |
| 2 ♡ | Pass | 3 ◊ | Pass |
| 3 ♡ | Pass | 4 ♡ | Pass |

As West you hold ♠ A 4   ♡ 6 4 2   ◊ K Q J 9 ♣ J 10 9 8.   What do you lead? A trump. The average player leads a club or a diamond. The expert who really listens to the bidding leads a trump to cut down dummy's ruffing power. Your club tricks aren't going to run away because the only place declarer can park his losing clubs is on dummy's diamond suit, which you have bottled up. The complete deal may well be as follows:

```
                    NORTH
                 ♠ 6
                 ♡ K 9 8
                 ◊ A 10 8 6 5 4 2
                 ♣ 7 3
    WEST                          EAST
 ♠ A 4                         ♠ J 10 9 8 5
 ♡ 6 4 2                       ♡ 5 3
 ◊ K Q J 9                     ◊ 3
 ♣ J 10 9 8                    ♣ K Q 6 5 2
                    SOUTH
                 ♠ K Q 7 3 2
                 ♡ A Q J 10 7
                 ◊ 7
                 ♣ A 4
```

If you lead a trump, declarer wins and will probably lead a spade to his king, which you win with the ace. At this point you lead another trump. Now South can make only nine tricks: five hearts in his hand, one spade ruff in dummy, one natural spade trick, and the two minor-suit aces. With any other opening lead, declarer can maneuver to get at least two spade ruffs and make his contract.

*Against six no-trump or any grand slam bid, it is usually right to make the safest lead in your hand.*

Example:

| SOUTH | WEST | NORTH | EAST |
|-------|------|-------|------|
| 2 ♡ | Pass | 3 ♡ | Pass |
| 7 ♡ | Pass | Pass | Pass |

As West you hold ♠ 9 4 2 ♡ 9 4 2 ◇ 9 4 2 ♣ 9 4 3 2. What do you lead? Life may look pretty grim at the moment, but keep a stiff upper lip and you may beat this hand yet. Declarer may be missing a queen somewhere for which he has a two-way finesse. He may misguess it, provided you don't let the cat out of the bag by leading that suit. Which queen does partner hold? You don't know. But you do know from the bidding that your team isn't going to win any trump tricks. The safest lead with this hand is therefore a trump.

## When Should You Lead a Singleton?

A singleton is a very aggressive and potentially danger-ous lead because it can damage your partner's hand severely. Yet the average player eagerly throws his single-ton upon the table without any forethought as to what it may accomplish. Here's an extreme example:

```
                    NORTH
                 ♠ J 8 6 5 2
                 ♡ A Q
                 ◇ J 8 4 3
                 ♣ A 2

      WEST                          EAST
   ♠ A 4 3                       ♠ —
   ♡ J 9 8 5 4                   ♡ 10 6 3 2
   ◇ 9                           ◇ K 10 6 2
   ♣ J 10 7 6                    ♣ 9 8 5 4 3

                    SOUTH
                 ♠ K Q 10 9 7
                 ♡ K 7
                 ◇ A Q 7 5
                 ♣ K Q
```

The bidding:

| SOUTH | WEST | NORTH | EAST |
|-------|------|-------|------|
| 1 ♠   | Pass | 3 ♠   | Pass |
| 4 NT  | Pass | 5 ♡   | Pass |
| 6 ♠   | Pass | Pass  | Pass |

West led the singleton diamond, dummy covered, and
South topped East's king with the ace. After drawing
trumps, declarer led the diamond eight from dummy and
easily brought home the whole suit. With any other lead,
declarer would probably have misguessed the diamond
situation and gone down.

Holding the spade ace himself, West had absolutely no
reason to make such a dangerous lead. He had nothing to
gain, because if East could get on lead to give him a ruff,
it would mean that the contract was already defeated. It's
very expensive to try for a set of two tricks at the risk of
letting declarer make a slam!

Suppose, however, that the bidding is the same as above
but West holds  ♠ 10 4 3  ♡ J 9 8 5 4  ◇ 9  ♣ J 10 7 6.
Now he has a good reason to lead the singleton. Partner

probably holds one ace. If it's the ace of diamonds or the ace of spades, West will get a chance to ruff a diamond return by partner and the slam is defeated. This is a fair shot and well worth the risk.

Against a game contract, the ideal time to lead a singleton is when you hold a sure trump entry plus an extra trump to ruff with, such as K x x, A x, or A x x. A singleton lead is less effective with a trump holding of K x or Q x x. Since a ruff may cost you a trump trick pickup a singleton lead is usually a poor choice when you have long trumps (four or more). It's better in this case to force declarer by leading your own long suit.

Example:

```
                    NORTH
                 ♠ 6 4 2
                 ♡ Q 10
                 ◊ J 7 5 3
                 ♣ A K Q J

       WEST                       EAST
    ♠ A 8 7 5                  ♠ 3
    ♡ 4                        ♡ A 7 6 5 3 2
    ◊ A Q 9 8 4                ◊ K 10 6 2
    ♣ 4 3 2                    ♣ 8 5

                    SOUTH
                 ♠ K Q J 10 9
                 ♡ K J 9 8
                 ◊ —
                 ♣ 10 9 7 6
```

The bidding:

| NORTH | EAST | SOUTH | WEST |
|-------|------|-------|------|
| 1 ♣   | Pass | 1 ♠   | Pass |
| 1 NT  | Pass | 3 ♡   | Pass |
| 3 ♠   | Pass | 4 ♠   | Pass |

Notice what happens if West opens has singleton heart. Even though he has the good fortune to find that partner has the ace and is able to give him a ruff, the defense gets only three tricks (heart ace, one ruff, and the spade ace) and declarer makes his contract. If, however, West leads the diamond ace originally, and the defense continues to lead diamonds every time it has the lead, the South hand will collapse under the pressure and four spades is defeated.

While we're on the subject of singletons, don't forget that it's sometimes a good idea to lead your partner's singleton.

Example:

```
                    NORTH
                  ♠ 10 5 2
                  ♡ A K 4
                  ◊ K J 10 2
                  ♣ K 3 2

      WEST                              EAST
    ♠ A 4                             ♠ 7 6 3
    ♡ 8 7 6 2                         ♡ Q J 9 5 3
    ◊ 9 6 4 3                         ◊ 7
    ♣ Q J 10                          ♣ 9 8 7 6

                    SOUTH
                  ♠ K Q J 9 8
                  ♡ 10
                  ◊ A Q 8 5
                  ♣ A 5 4
```

The bidding:

| NORTH | EAST | SOUTH | WEST |
|-------|------|-------|------|
| 1 ◊   | Pass | 1 ♠   | Pass |
| 1 NT  | Pass | 3 ◊   | Pass |
| 3 ♠   | Pass | 6 ♠   | Pass |
| Pass  | Pass |       |      |

If West doesn't stop to think, he'll automatically lead the club queen, and declarer makes the slam. If West uses his head, he'll lead a diamond, grab the spade ace at the first opportunity, and lead another diamond for partner to ruff. This defeats the contract.

·

### Is It Better to Lead Partner's Suit or Your Own Suit?

There are, naturally, many factors involved in making the right decision: your holding in partner's suit, the circumstances under which partner bid, the texture of your own suit, etc. After weighing all the available evidence, if you're still in doubt I suggest you lead partner's suit. The reason is this. If you lead your own suit and it turns out to be wrong, partner, being only human, is going to be annoyed that you didn't lead his suit. However, if you lead his suit and it turns out to be wrong, he'll be relatively understanding. At least you'll have preserved the partnership harmony.

### Lead-Directing Doubles

Sometimes a defender will have the opportunity during the auction to make a lead-directing double. A double of an artificial bid is a case in point.

Example:

| SOUTH | WEST | NORTH | EAST |
|-------|------|-------|------|
| 1 NT | Pass | 2 ♣ | Double |
| 2 ♠ | Pass | 3 NT | Pass |
| Pass | Pass | | |

NOTE: The two-club bid is the Stayman Convention (See Chapter 11). East may hold something like K Q J 10 x of clubs. By doubling the artificial Stayman bid, East is able to indicate to his partner the best suit to attack.

Occasionally the fact that partner did not make a certain double must also be considered.

Example:

| SOUTH | WEST | NORTH | EAST |
|-------|------|-------|------|
| 1 ♠ | Pass | 3 ♠ | Pass |
| 4 NT | Pass | 5 ◇ | Pass |
| 6 ♠ | Pass | Pass | Pass |

In choosing his opening lead, West must give some slight weight to the fact that East had a chance to double five diamonds for a lead and did not do so.

A double of a three no-trump contract usually calls for a specific lead.

Example 1.

| NORTH | EAST | SOUTH | WEST |
|-------|------|-------|------|
| 1 ♡ | 1 ♠ | 2 NT | Pass |
| 3 NT | Double | Pass | Pass |
| Pass | | | |

Here, East is doubling to ensure that his partner leads a spade. Without the double, West might be tempted to experiment with some other suit, particularly if he has only a singleton spade. The double says, "Partner, if you lead a spade I can defeat three no-trump in my own hand."

Example 2.

| SOUTH | WEST | NORTH | EAST |
|-------|------|-------|------|
| 1 ♣ | 1 ♡ | 1 ♠ | Pass |
| 1 NT | Pass | 3 NT | Double |
| Pass | Pass | Pass | |

This time, East's double asks partner to lead hearts, his own suit. East almost certainly has a high heart honor. Without the double, West might be afraid to lead away from his heart tenace.

Example 3.

| SOUTH | WEST | NORTH | EAST |
|-------|------|-------|------|
| 1 ◇ | Pass | 1 ♡ | Pass |
| 3 NT | Pass | Pass | Double |
| Pass | Pass | Pass | |

In this case, East is shouting for a lead of dummy's suit. North has probably responded one heart on something like J x x x, shutting out East's natural overcall. Remember, East couldn't double one heart to show hearts because a double of a low-level contract when partner has never bid is primarily for a take-out.

## The Lightner Slam Double

A double of a voluntarily bid slam is always lead-directing. This double, known as the Lightner Slam Double after its inventor, calls for an *unusual* lead. The idea is this: It doesn't pay to double a slam simply because you think you can beat it. The extra fifty or one hundred points you stand to gain are peanuts in comparison to what you stand to lose if, thanks to your double, declarer is able to locate the cards and fulfill his contract. The double is therefore more valuable as a lead-directing device. It says, "Partner, do *not* make the expected opening lead. I have a surprise holding (probably a void) in a suit that you would not normally lead."

Example 1.

| EAST | SOUTH | WEST | NORTH |
|------|-------|------|-------|
| 1 ♠ | 3 ♡ | Pass | 6 ♡ |
| Double | Pass | Pass | Pass |

If East had not doubled, West would have been expected to lead a spade. By doubling, East is desperately asking West *not* to lead a spade. He is probably void in clubs or diamonds, and West should be able to tell which by looking at his own distribution.

Example 2.

| SOUTH | WEST | NORTH | EAST |
|-------|------|-------|------|
| 1 ♠ | Pass | 2 ♣ | Pass |
| 3 ♠ | Pass | 6 ♠ | Double |
| Pass | Pass | Pass | |

165

This time, if East had not doubled, West would be expected to lead a diamond or a heart, the two unbid suits. The double here specifically calls for a club lead, dummy's suit.

The Lightner Slam Double calls for an unusual lead: usually dummy's suit if he has bid one, never trumps, and never the suit which the opening leader might be expected to lead if it hadn't been for the double.

Summing up: Remember there are two problems facing the opening leader: which suit to lead and which card within the suit to select. The proper card to select is very easy. Simply follow the rules given at the beginning of this chapter. Choosing the right suit to lead can be difficult. Sometimes partner will be able to direct your lead with a judicious double. For the most part, however, you'll have to weigh all the available evidence and then use your best judgment.


## QUIZ ON OPENING LEADS

Warning! Just because you have read this chapter carefully, doesn't mean you can sit back and relax and expect to do well on this quiz. This is a tough quiz. If you get more than half the questions right you have done well. If you get them all right, I shall expect to see you in the finals of next year's National Blue Ribbon Championship.

Remember, no one can teach you what to lead on every deal. You must develop the habit of *picturing all four hands* and *thinking for yourself.*

In each of the following hands you are West. What should you lead, and why?

1.
| SOUTH | WEST | NORTH | EAST |
|-------|------|-------|------|
| 1 ◇ | Double | Pass | Pass |
| Pass | | | |

You hold ♠ A Q 6 2 ♡ Q J 10 7 ◇ 4 ♣ K Q 10 4.

2.

| SOUTH | WEST | NORTH | EAST |
|-------|------|-------|------|
| 1 ♣ | Pass | 3 ♣ | Pass |
| 3 ♡ | Pass | 3 ♠ | Pass |
| 4 ♣ | Pass | 5 ♣ | Pass |
| Pass | Pass | | |

You hold ♠ J 10 8 ♡ K 9 5 3 ◊ A Q 4 3 ♣ 8 7.

3.

| SOUTH | WEST | NORTH | EAST |
|-------|------|-------|------|
| 1 ♠ | Pass | 3 ♠ | Pass |
| 7 ♠ | Pass | Pass | Pass |

You hold ♠ 4 ♡ J 6 2 ◊ J 8 7 2 ♣ J 8 6 4 2.

4.

| SOUTH | WEST | NORTH | EAST |
|-------|------|-------|------|
| 1 ♡ | Pass | 1 NT | Pass |
| 2 ◊ | Pass | 3 ◊ | Pass |
| Pass | Pass | | |

You hold ♠ A Q 5 ♡ J ◊ J 6 4 3 2 ♣ K 10 5 4.

5.

| SOUTH | WEST | NORTH | EAST |
|-------|------|-------|------|
| 1 NT | Pass | 3 NT | Pass |
| Pass | Pass | | |

You hold ♠ K 4 ♡ K J 7 5 2 ◊ Q 5 3 ♣ 10 8 2.

6.

| SOUTH | WEST | NORTH | EAST |
|-------|------|-------|------|
| 2 NT | Pass | Pass | Pass |

You hold ♠ 10 9 2 ♡ K J 6 2 ◊ Q 7 3 2 ♣ 4 3.

7.

| SOUTH | WEST | NORTH | EAST |
|-------|------|-------|------|
| | | 1 NT | 2 ♡ |
| 3 ♠ | Pass | 4 ♠ | Pass |
| 6 ♠ | Pass | Pass | Double |
| Pass | Pass | Pass | |

You hold ♠ 10 2 ♡ J 10 3 ◊ Q 9 6 4 3 2 ♣ J 5.

8.

| SOUTH | WEST | NORTH | EAST |
|-------|------|-------|------|
| 1 NT | Pass | 3 NT | Double |
| Pass | Pass | Pass | |

You hold ♠ 10 6 4 3 ♡ 7 ◊ 8 5 4 2 ♣ J 6 4 3.

**Answers to Quiz**

1. The diamond four. First let's picture partner's hand. Your take-out double of one diamond asked him to choose between spades, hearts, and clubs. If he hasn't got four cards in one of these suits he may have to bid a three-card suit. But partner has decided to *override* you. Why? Because he thinks he can set one diamond. In fact, he expects to score more defending at one diamond than playing in any other spot. If he wants to play in diamonds, knowing that the trumps are stacked over him (on his left), his diamond suit must be pretty solid and at least five cards long. Now look at things from declarer's point of view. In addition to the high cards in his hand, he has several little diamonds with which he's hoping to win tricks by ruffing. To stop him from doing this you must *draw his trumps*. And, the sooner you get started the better. *When partner leaves in your take-out double of a one bid he's hoping for a trump lead.*

2. The diamond ace. Did you hear anyone bid no-trump? North and South passed the ball back and forth for quite a while, each trying to get the other fellow to bid no-trump. (They know it's easier to make nine tricks in no-trump than eleven tricks in a minor suit.) But neither of them bid no-trump because neither of them had a diamond stopper. Thus, partner almost surely has the diamond king, and the defense will do well to cash as many diamond tricks as possible. If you don't cash the diamonds immediately, there's a chance declarer may be able to get rid of his diamond losers on dummy's spade winners.

3. The club four. Against any grand slam, you should make the safest possible lead. The singleton trump is dangerous because partner might hold Q x x. The heart, diamond, and club leads are also slightly risky because you may be setting up a side suit for declarer. Sacrificing your fourth-round stopper in clubs is the *least risky* because you have so many it's unlikely that either opponent has four of them.

4. A small diamond. It is almost certain that North and South each have four diamonds. Declarer is obviously short of black cards, and dummy is probably short of hearts. By cross-ruffing the hand, declarer can take eight tricks in trumps alone if they are never led. Each time you lead a trump you hold declarer to one less trick!

5. The heart five. The best way to develop five tricks here is to attack with your longest suit.

6. The spade ten. You should expect to set this contract. Without any entries to dummy, declarer won't be able to finesse or even lead up to his honors. There's no point in making an especially risky lead here.

7. The diamond four. Partner is calling for an unusual lead, *not* hearts and *not* trumps. The chances are that he's void of diamonds.

8. The heart seven. This is an unusual situation. Even if partner has about an opening bid himself, this would be a very poor reason to double and locate all the cards for declarer. It's more likely that partner has a suit somewhere, possibly K Q J 10 x, and at least one entry on the side. (Remember, he never got a chance to bid except at the four level.) By doubling, he's begging you to lead his suit. You know, of course, that his suit is hearts. On the bidding, it's unlikely that North and South have an eight-card major-suit fit. Thus, East should have five or more hearts.

Whether or not you did well on these questions is unimportant, because they were only partially based on the material in the chapter. The primary object of this quiz was to introduce some fresh ideas on opening leads. While you were reading the answers, were you able to say, even once, "Well, I never considered that angle before"? If so, the quiz was a success, and you are that much better equipped to fire the opening salvo of the defense.

## 13

# The Art of Signaling

Ever since Lord Henry Bentinck first invented the high-low signal in 1834, experienced players have been using their "immaterial" cards to send messages back and forth across the table. Take the following example:

DUMMY

◇ A 6 3

WEST

◇ K 10 7 5

EAST

◇ Q 8 4 2

DECLARER

◇ J 9

Against a no-trump contract, West leads the diamond five. If dummy plays low, East naturally plays the queen in an attempt to win the trick. If dummy plays the ace, however, East has a choice of three "immaterial" cards to play: the eight, the four, or the two. In a situation like this, a beginner would probably play the two simply because it's his smallest card. At any rate, no special meaning could be attached to his choice. An experienced player would play the eight as a signal to his partner that he wanted the suit continued.

Today, a signal can convey any one of three separate messages depending on the situation in which it is used.

The three signals available are:

1. the come-on signal
2. the count signal
3. the suit-preference signal

Although the student soon learns to use these signals, he rarely is taught *which signal applies when*. Consequently, he uses them all indiscriminately. By the time he becomes a fairly sophisticated player in other respects, his defense has become a complete hodgepodge. Even among good players, one often hears remarks like these:

First player: "Why didn't you continue hearts, partner? I gave you the ten!"

Partner: "It looked like a suit-preference signal to me. I thought you wanted a spade shift." Or,

First player: "Why did you give me that come-on signal in clubs?"

Partner: "That was no come-on signal! I was just trying to give you the count."

What's the solution to all this confusion? A simple bit of old-fashioned organization! Let's start at the beginning.

## The Come-on Signal

The most important signal, and the first signal the beginner learns, is the come-on signal. The principle is this. *Whenever partner leads to a trick and you have an opportunity to signal, you should play a high card if you want the suit continued and a low card if you don't want it continued.*

Example 1.

                    NORTH
                    ♠ K 6 2
                    ♡ 10 7
                    ◊ K 10 9 7 2
                    ♣ A 8 4

        WEST                         EAST
     ♠ 10 9 7                     ♠ J 8 4 3
     ♡ A K 5                      ♡ Q 8 6 4 2
     ◊ 8 6 4                      ◊ 5 3
     ♣ J 9 6 3                    ♣ Q 10

                    SOUTH
                    ♠ A Q 5
                    ♡ J 9 3
                    ◊ A Q J
                    ♣ K 7 6 2

The bidding:

| SOUTH | WEST | NORTH | EAST |
|-------|------|-------|------|
| 1 NT  | Pass | 3 NT  | Pass |
| Pass  | Pass |       |      |

Against three no-trump, West leads the king of hearts.
East is delighted with this suit and should play the eight to
encourage partner to continue. Actually, East has four
gradations of signal available to him on this trick, the eight,
six, four, or two. Here are the approximate meanings of
each:

The two: "Stop leading hearts."
The four: "I can tolerate a heart continuation."
The six: "Please continue hearts."
The eight: "FOR THE LOVE OF MIKE LEAD ANOTHER
HEART!"

In this case, East is sure he wants hearts continued so he
plays the highest card he can afford, the eight. When you're
sure you want something, don't whisper, SHOUT!

Example 2.

```
                    NORTH
                 ♠ Q 10 5 4
                 ♡ Q 5 3
                 ◇ K Q 6
                 ♣ K Q 6

    WEST                          EAST
 ♠ A K 7 2                     ♠ 8 3
 ♡ 10 4                        ♡ 9 7 2
 ◇ 10 9 7                      ◇ J 8 5 4
 ♣ A 5 4 2                     ♣ J 8 7 3

                    SOUTH
                 ♠ J 9 6
                 ♡ A K J 8 6
                 ◇ A 3 2
                 ♣ 10 9
```

The bidding:

| SOUTH | WEST | NORTH | EAST |
|-------|------|-------|------|
| 1 ♡   | Pass | 2 NT  | Pass |
| 3 ♡   | Pass | 4 ♡   | Pass |
| Pass  | Pass |       |      |

Against four hearts, West leads the spade king, on which East should play the eight. He wants the suit continued. West obligingly leads the ace and another spade for East to ruff. Now declarer can't make his contract. If East had played the spade three at trick one, West might have shifted to some other suit and declarer would have made four hearts.

Notice in both of these examples, the come-on signal applied when the signaler's *partner* led to the trick involved.

There's another way in which this signal is used and that is in discarding. *A player's first discard in any suit may be a signal.*

Example 3.

```
                    NORTH
                    ♠ K Q J 10 4 2
                    ♡ 6 3 2
                    ◇ 7 4
                    ♣ K 10

    WEST                              EAST
    ♠ A 7 4                           ♠ 5 3
    ♡ 7 5                             ♡ A K Q J
    ◇ Q 8 5                           ◇ 6 3 2
    ♣ J 9 7 6 5                       ♣ 8 4 3 2

                    SOUTH
                    ♠ 9 8
                    ♡ 10 9 8 4
                    ◇ A K J 10 9
                    ♣ A Q
```

The bidding:

| NORTH | EAST | SOUTH | WEST |
|-------|------|-------|------|
| 3 ♠   | Pass | 3 NT  | Pass |
| Pass  | Pass |       |      |

Against three no-trump, West leads the club six. Dummy
plays the ten, West plays the two, a negative signal meaning, "Don't continue clubs," and declarer wins with the
ace. Declarer now attacks spades and West holds off until
the third round, giving East a chance to make one discard.
East is naturally anxious for his partner to shift to a heart,
but unfortunately he can't spare one to signal with. The
best he can do is to throw the two of diamonds, another
negative signal meaning, "Don't lead diamonds." If West
is alert he will now switch to a heart and defeat the
contract.


**The Count Signal**

When declarer (or dummy) leads a suit, the come-on
signal becomes relatively useless. After all, if *declarer* is
voluntarily attacking a suit, it's hardly likely that a *de-*

*fender* also wants to attack it. Confucius say, "Two teams lead same suit, one team crazy." Therefore, when declarer leads a suit it has been found much more valuable for the defenders to give count. The general rule is this: *when declarer leads a plain suit (any suit except trumps), a defender should echo (play high-low) to indicate that he holds an even number of cards in the suit, and he should follow from the bottom up to indicate that he holds an odd number of cards.* The count signal always applies to the number of cards originally held in the suit.

Here's a very common example:

Example 4.

```
                     NORTH
                  ♠ K Q J 10 5
                  ♡ 6 5
                  ◇ 4 3 2
                  ♣ 8 5 4

    WEST                              EAST
 ♠ 9 3 2                           ♠ A 7 4
 ♡ K 10 8 7 3                      ♡ J 9
 ◇ Q 5                             ◇ K J 8 7 6
 ♣ 10 9 7                          ♣ 6 3 2

                     SOUTH
                  ♠ 8 6
                  ♡ A Q 4 2
                  ◇ A 10 9
                  ♣ A K Q J
```

The bidding:

| SOUTH | WEST | NORTH | EAST |
|-------|------|-------|------|
| 1 ♣   | Pass | 1 ♠   | Pass |
| 3 NT  | Pass | Pass  | Pass |

Against three no-trump, West leads the heart seven, East plays the jack, and South wins with the queen. At the second trick, declarer leads a spade. West follows with the two to show partner that he was dealt an *odd* number of

175

spades. East is now aware that declarer has two spades in his hand so he holds up once with his ace. Notice that if East takes the first spade trick, declarer will make five no-trump. And if he holds up twice, declarer will make three no-trump. But, by ducking once and winning the second spade lead, East sets the contract!

Here's a more advanced example:

Example 5.

<table>
<tr><td></td><td>NORTH</td><td></td></tr>
<tr><td></td><td>♠ A Q</td><td></td></tr>
<tr><td></td><td>♡ 10 9 8 7 6 4</td><td></td></tr>
<tr><td></td><td>◇ 10 9 5</td><td></td></tr>
<tr><td></td><td>♣ 7 5</td><td></td></tr>
</table>

| WEST | EAST |
|------|------|
| ♠ 9 8 7 | ♠ 10 6 5 4 2 |
| ♡ 5 | ♡ A 3 2 |
| ◇ J 8 7 6 3 | ◇ 2 |
| ♣ 10 9 6 3 | ♣ K 8 4 2 |

<table>
<tr><td>SOUTH</td></tr>
<tr><td>♠ K J 3</td></tr>
<tr><td>♡ K Q J</td></tr>
<tr><td>◇ A K Q 4</td></tr>
<tr><td>♣ A Q J</td></tr>
</table>

The bidding:

| SOUTH | WEST | NORTH | EAST |
|-------|------|-------|------|
| 2 ♣ | Pass | 2 ♡ | Pass |
| 4 NT | Pass | 5 ◇ | Pass |
| 6 NT | Pass | Pass | Pass |

NOTE: South's two-club bid is artificial.

Against six no-trump, West leads the nine of spades. Declarer wins in dummy and takes a club finesse. When this holds, he leads the heart king. East wins and returns a spade, knocking out dummy's last entry. Now, declarer apparently must go down because he has a little diamond left in his hand and no way to get to dummy to dispose of it on the good hearts. But look what happens! After winning the second spade in dummy, declarer takes another club finesse and then cashes the queen and jack of hearts and the king of spades. West has to make two discards. He can spare one diamond, but what else should he throw? Did declarer have four clubs originally, or four diamonds?

The average West would guess wrong about half the time and would present declarer with his slam. If East and West are good players, however, they have no trouble with this hand. When clubs are led, East follows first with the four and then with the two. West now knows his partner had an even number of clubs originally, and easily figures that it's safe for him to throw a club.

Suppose the cards had been divided like this:

NORTH
♠ A Q
♡ 10 9 8 7 6 4
◇ 10 9 5
♣ 7 5

WEST
♠ 9 8 7
♡ 5
◇ J 8 7 6 3
♣ 10 9 6 3

EAST
♠ 10 6 5 4 2
♡ A 3 2
◇ 4 2
♣ K 4 2

SOUTH
♠ K J 3
♡ K Q J
◇ A K Q
♣ A Q J 8

On the first lead of clubs, East would follow with the two. The next time he'd play the four. Now West would know his partner had an odd number of clubs originally. He'd play declarer for four clubs and defeat the slam by discarding another diamond.

Some players worry that if they always show count,

they'll unwittingly help declarer more than partner. Remember this: defense is a much more difficult science than dummy play because a defender sees only thirteen of his side's twenty-six cards. Therefore, in most cases, the defenders stand to gain more from partner's signals than does declarer.

Many players don't realize that the count signal may sometimes be used in discarding. Of course the *come-on* signal is the most important, and a player's *first* discard in any suit is for *come-on*. However, *when come-on can't possibly apply, or has already been applied, the count signal takes over*.

For example, suppose you hold K Q 10 9 8 4 2 of hearts. Spades are trump, and when declarer runs the trump suit you are forced to make three heart discards. Your first discard would naturally be the heart ten, a come-on signal meaning, "I'm loaded in hearts, partner." Your next two discards would be the heart two and then the four, a count signal meaning, "I originally held an odd number of hearts, partner." If your heart holding had been K Q 10 9 6 2, you'd throw the ten first for come-on. Next you'd echo with the six and then the two, a count signal meaning, "I was dealt an even number of hearts, partner."

This procedure is called giving "original count." However some experts nowadays give "present count." If they have four cards *remaining* in a suit they will play high, and so on. A regular partnership should discuss this point.

Here is a hand where beautiful defense by a pair of young players was ruined by a lack of understanding of this discarding principle:

Example 6.

                        NORTH
                        ♠ A K 3 2
                        ♡ 7 4 3 2
                        ◊ 9 7
                        ♣ J 5 4

    WEST                                    EAST
    ♠ 10 4                                  ♠ 8 5 4
    ♡ K 6 5                                 ♡ 9 8
    ◊ 10 6 3 2                              ◊ Q 8 5 4
    ♣ 7 6 3 2                               ♣ Q 10 9 8

                        SOUTH
                        ♠ Q J 7 6
                        ♡ A Q J 10
                        ◊ A K J
                        ♣ A K

The bidding:

| SOUTH | WEST | NORTH | EAST |
|-------|------|-------|------|
| 2 ♣ | Pass | 2 ♠ | Pass |
| 4 NT | Pass | 5 ◊ | Pass |
| 5 NT | Pass | 6 ◊ | Pass |
| 6 NT | Pass | Pass | Pass |

At many tables, North-South played six of a major suit for a score of 980. At other tables, South played six no-trump. These declarers used one spade entry to finesse the heart, and when this lost they used the other entry to finesse the diamond. Luckily this succeeded, and they scored 990.

At the table where our young players were East-West, the bidding went as shown in the diagram. Declarer won the first trick with the spade ace and took the heart finesse on which West smoothly played low. Happily, declarer returned to the spade king and led another heart. This time, to his horror, the finesse lost and back came a third heart. It was now too late to try the diamond finesse, and as the cards lay declarer had to go down. West had made a fine play and a logical one. He had induced South to squander dummy's last entry on a losing heart finesse instead of some other finesse which West knew must win.

But look what happened! Declarer won the third heart in his hand. He then cashed the other heart and the remaining spades on which East had to make three discards. He could spare one diamond and one club, but on the last spade he had to unguard one of his queens and he guessed wrong! So this declarer made 990 points also, and West's fine play went for naught.

Look how easy it would have been for East to discard correctly if West had signaled properly. West has three discards to make before East is forced to make his fateful decision. His first discard is naturally the club two. This means simply, "I have nothing in clubs" (negative signal). His next two discards are the seven and then the three of clubs. This says, "I had an even number of clubs originally" (count signal). East would now have no trouble reading declarer for the ace and king of clubs alone. He would discard a club and defeat the slam.

## The Trump Echo

In the trump suit, the count signal is reversed. *Following to trumps, a defender should echo with an odd number of trumps in his hand, and follow suit normally with an even number.*

This may seem strange at first, but it is perfectly normal if the evolution of the signal is considered. All signals were originally attention getters. Playing high-low in trumps was first used to alert partner of a third trump and a desire to ruff something. There are still many good players today who echo with three trumps only when they can ruff something. In order to give partner the maximum assistance in counting the hand, however, it's best to echo with an odd number of trumps whenever feasible.

Here's an example of the value of the trump echo:

Example 7.

```
                    NORTH
                  ♠ Q J 6 4
                  ♡ K 6 4 2
                  ◊ A 8 5
                  ♣ A 2

     WEST                          EAST
   ♠ 8 5 3                       ♠ A
   ♡ 3                           ♡ A 10 9 7 5
   ◊ J 7 6 3 2                   ◊ K Q 10 9
   ♣ 10 9 6 5                    ♣ 8 7 4

                    SOUTH
                  ♠ K 10 9 7 2
                  ♡ Q J 8
                  ◊ 4
                  ♣ K Q J 3
```

The bidding:

| EAST | SOUTH | WEST | NORTH |
|------|-------|------|-------|
| 1 ♡ | 1 ♠ | Pass | 4 ♠ |
| Pass | Pass | Pass | |

East wins the first trick with the ace of hearts. He returns the ten, which West ruffs with the spade *five*. West returns a diamond, and dummy hops up with the ace and leads a trump. East plays the ace and West the *three*. At this point, should East try to cash the diamond king for the setting trick, or should he try to give partner another ruff? He is not sure that the diamond king will live, but he knows from West's echo in spades that his partner has another trump. So, he leads a heart and defeats the contract.

### The Suit-Preference Signal

The suit-preference signal occurs primarily in belated lead situations, that is, in leads other than the opening lead. The principle is this: a defender leads a *high* card of one suit to indicate that his entry is in the *higher ranking* of two other suits. He leads a *low* card to indicate that his entry is in the *lower ranking* of two other suits.

The suit-preference signal is most often used where a ruff is involved.

Example 8.

```
                    NORTH
                  ♠ K J 9
                  ♡ K Q J 7 3
                  ◇ J 7
                  ♣ J 7 6

     WEST                           EAST
   ♠ 10 6                         ♠ 3 2
   ♡ 4                            ♡ A 10 8 2
   ◇ Q 10 9 8 4                   ◇ A 6 3 2
   ♣ Q 10 9 5 2                   ♣ K 8 3

                    SOUTH
                  ♠ A Q 8 7 5 4
                  ♡ 9 6 5
                  ◇ K 5
                  ♣ A 4
```

The bidding:

| SOUTH | WEST | NORTH | EAST |
|-------|------|-------|------|
| 1 ♠   | Pass | 2 ♡   | Pass |
| 2 ♠   | Pass | 4 ♠   | Pass |
| Pass  | Pass |       |      |

Against four spades, West leads his singleton heart, and East wins with the ace. East now leads back his heart ten (his highest) to tell partner to return a diamond, the higher ranking of the two side suits. (For the purpose of determining which two suits apply, the trump suit is ignored.) West ruffs the heart ten and obligingly returns a diamond to his partner's ace. East returns another heart, and the contract is defeated.

Here is another example of suit preference at work:

Example 9.

```
                    NORTH
                    ♠ 9 8 5
                    ♡ Q 3
                    ◊ K Q J 5 4 3
                    ♣ J 6

    WEST                                EAST
♠ Q 10 7 3 2                        ♠ A 4
♡ A 9 6                             ♡ 10 8 5 4 2
◊ 8 6 2                             ◊ A
♣ 9 3                              ♣ 10 8 5 4 2

                    SOUTH
                    ♠ K J 6
                    ♡ K J 7
                    ◊ 10 9 7
                    ♣ A K Q 7
```

The bidding:

| SOUTH | WEST | NORTH | EAST |
|-------|------|-------|------|
| 1 NT  | Pass | 3 NT  | Pass |
| Pass  | Pass |       |      |

Against a contract of three no-trump, West leads the spade three. East wins with the ace and returns the four. South plays the jack on the second trick and West wins with the queen. At this point West can knock out declarer's spade king with any one of his three remaining spades: the ten, the seven, or the two. He should select the ten, his highest spade, so that when East wins his diamond ace, he'll return a heart, the *higher ranking* of the two possible suits in which West could have an entry.

Without the suit-preference signal, when East took his diamond ace he'd face a complete guess as to whether to return a club or a heart. If he returns a club, declarer will make four no-trump. Thanks to the suit-preference signal, East returns a heart and defeats the contract two tricks.

The suit-preference signal is used most frequently in belated lead situations like the two examples just given.

It can also apply, occasionally, on the opening lead *provided it cannot possibly be interpreted as a normal fourth best*.

Example 10.

```
                    NORTH
                  ♠ A Q 7 5
                  ♡ 9
                  ◇ K J 9 7
                  ♣ K Q 10 9

      WEST                           EAST
    ♠ 9 8                          ♠ 3
    ♡ K Q J 8 7 6 2                ♡ A 10 4 3
    ◇ 10 5 4 2                     ◇ Q 8 6 3
    ♣ —                            ♣ J 5 4 3

                    SOUTH
                  ♠ K J 10 6 4 2
                  ♡ 5
                  ◇ A
                  ♣ A 8 7 6 2
```

The bidding:

| WEST | NORTH | EAST | SOUTH |
|------|-------|------|-------|
| 3 ♡ | Double | 4 ♡ | 6 ♠ |
| Pass | Pass | Pass | |

West leads the heart two. Under normal circumstances this would probably mean that West was leading fourth best from a four-card suit. Here, such an interpretation is impossible in view of West's opening bid of three hearts. East, therefore, correctly interprets the heart two as calling for a return of the lower-ranking suit. Accordingly, East takes the heart ace and leads back a club to defeat the slam.

Very occasionally a situation will arise where the suit-preference signal can be applied by a defender who does not have the lead. This can occur *only* if the normal meaning of the signal is obviously impossible.

Example 11.

```
                    NORTH
                 ♠ 10
                 ♡ J 10 3
                 ◇ 9 8 6 2
                 ♣ K Q 10 9 4

  WEST                              EAST
♠ A Q 6 5 4 3                    ♠ 2
♡ A Q 7                          ♡ K 8 6 5 4 2
◇ 4                              ◇ 10 7 3
♣ J 7 3                          ♣ 8 6 5

                    SOUTH
                 ♠ K J 9 8 7
                 ♡ 9
                 ◇ A K Q J 5
                 ♣ A 2
```

The bidding:

| WEST | NORTH | EAST | SOUTH |
|------|-------|------|-------|
| 1 ♠ | Pass | Pass | 3 ◇ |
| Pass | Pass | 3 ♡ | 4 ◇ |
| 4 ♡ | 5 ◇ | Pass | Pass |
| Pass | | | |

Against five diamonds, West led the spade ace. East regretted that his singleton was the lowly deuce. West shifted to the heart ace at trick two, and East faced the problem of how to get his partner to switch back to spades. He solved it by throwing the heart king under the ace! Ordinarily this would be a strong come-on signal in hearts. But here, the heart situation was such that once East had abandoned his king, West could no longer afford to lead the suit. West correctly interpreted this dramatic jettison as a desperate suit-preference signal for the higher suit. He led another spade and defeated the contract.

We've now covered the three available signals: *the come-on signal, the count signal*, and *the suit-preference signal*. It is important to remember that a signal can have only one meaning, depending on the circumstances under which it occurs. In this way, partner will always interpret your signal correctly, and the way will be paved for a smooth defense.

Review:
1. When following to a suit *led by partner*, the come-on signal applies.
2. When following to a suit *led by declarer*, the count signal applies.
3. When discarding, the come-on signal applies *first*. If come-on cannot apply, or has already been applied, the count signal takes over.
4. The suit-preference signal occurs primarily in belated lead situations. It can apply elsewhere *only* if another meaning is impossible.

## Signaling with an Honor

Obviously, a signal shouldn't be made with a card which a defender can't afford to part with. For this reason, a player rarely signals with a high honor unless he holds the honor just below it. This principle can be put to good use in the following kind of situation:

Example 12.

```
                    NORTH
                  ♠ 10 6
                  ♡ 4 2
                  ◇ 9 7 2
                  ♣ A K Q 6 5 4

     WEST                          EAST
   ♠ 9 8                         ♠ 7
   ♡ A K 6                       ♡ Q J 10 9 7 3
   ◇ A Q 6 3                     ◇ J 10 8 5
   ♣ 10 9 3 2                    ♣ 8 7

                    SOUTH
                  ♠ A K Q J 5 4 3 2
                  ♡ 8 5
                  ◇ K 4
                  ♣ J
```

The bidding:

| SOUTH | WEST | NORTH | EAST |
|-------|------|-------|------|
| 4 ♠   | Pass | Pass  | Pass |

West opens the king of hearts, on which partner drops the queen (a come-on signal which also shows possession of the heart jack). West now knows that it's safe to lead his small heart at trick two. East wins and returns a diamond, and the defense takes the first four tricks.

A come-on signal with any honor card denies possession of the honor just above it. A classic example of this occurs in the following hand:

Example 13.

```
                    NORTH
                    ♠ 8 7 5
                    ♡ A 9 2
                    ◇ Q 8 4
                    ♣ A K 8 2

   WEST                              EAST
   ♠ J 10 9 3                        ♠ K Q 2
   ♡ 7 5                             ♡ 6 4
   ◇ A 6 3                           ◇ K 10 9 7 2
   ♣ J 9 5 4                         ♣ Q 7 3

                    SOUTH
                    ♠ A 6 4
                    ♡ K Q J 10 8 3
                    ◇ J 5
                    ♣ 10 6
```

The bidding:

| NORTH | EAST | SOUTH | WEST |
|-------|------|-------|------|
| 1 ♣ | 1 ◇ | 1 ♡ | Pass |
| 1 NT | Pass | 3 ♡ | Pass |
| 4 ♡ | Pass | Pass | Pass |

Against four hearts, West led the ace of diamonds on which East played the ten, an obvious come-on signal but denying the jack. If West had held only two diamonds, he would have continued the suit and ruffed the third round. West realized, however, that South had the diamond jack and that dummy's diamond queen would soon provide a parking place for one of declarer's losers. So, at trick two he switched to spades. The defense won two spade tricks and two diamond tricks to beat the contract. Notice that if West had blindly obeyed his partner's come-on signal, declarer would have made four hearts.

#### How to Cancel a Come-on Signal

Sometimes a defender may wish to cancel a come-on signal. Suppose, for example, against a contract of four hearts the spades are distributed like this:

DUMMY

♠ 6 4

PARTNER                              YOU

♠ A K J 5 3                    ♠ Q 10 8 2

DECLARER

♠ 9 7

Your partner leads the king of spades and you play the eight to encourage him to cash his ace. When he continues with the ace, you now play the ten, *a higher card than the one you signaled with originally*. This asks him not to lead a third round. If you played the two on the ace, completing the echo, partner might lead another spade, which could be disastrous.

## Signals by Declarer

It may surprise many players to know that it is generally to the advantage of declarer to signal for come-on in exactly the same manner as though he were a defender.

DUMMY

◇ 8 7 4

WEST                              EAST

◇ K Q 10 9                    ◇ 6 3

DECLARER

◇ A J 5 2

Against a no-trump contract, West leads the king of diamonds and the suit is distributed as above. East naturally plays the three, his smallest card, to stop partner from continuing. However, declarer wants West to lead another diamond, so he should play the *five*, not the *two*. West will now notice that the two is missing and he may think his partner is encouraging him with the three from a holding of A 3 2 or J 3 2. If West leads another diamond, declarer will make two diamond tricks. Notice that if declarer plays the two on the first trick, West can easily read partner's three as a discouraging card. He will discontinue the suit, and declarer will never make more than one diamond trick.

The converse is also true. Declarer should play his smallest card when he doesn't want a suit continued.

DUMMY
♡ Q 10 6 5

WEST                       EAST
♡ A K 8 7                ♡ 4 2

DECLARER
♡ J 9 3

Against a spade contract, West leads the heart king and East starts an echo with the four spot, hoping to ruff the third round. Declarer's best chance to stop West from continuing the suit is to play the three. West may now think his partner has jack-nine-four, and may shift to another suit. If declarer plays the nine or the jack on the first trick, West will be able to read his partner's holding as either the four-three or the four-two or the singleton four spot and will continue the suit.

As a general rule, the best way to disrupt the defenders' signals is for declarer to signal in the same way himself: *high* when he wants a suit continued, and *low* when he doesn't.

# QUIZ ON SIGNALING

1.

DUMMY
♠ 7 5 4
♡ K 6 3
♦ K Q J 10
♣ 10 4 2

YOU                                        PARTNER
♠ 10 9 8 6 3 2                             ?
♡ 7
♦ 7 6 5 2
♣ Q 7

DECLARER
?

The bidding:

| SOUTH | WEST | NORTH | EAST |
|-------|------|-------|------|
| 1 ♣   | Pass | 1 ♦   | Pass |
| 2 NT  | Pass | 3 NT  | Pass |
| Pass  | Pass |       |      |

Against three no-trump, you lead the spade ten, partner plays the queen, and declarer wins with the king. At trick two, declarer leads a low diamond. Which diamond do you play?

**2.**

              DUMMY
              ♠ Q 10 6 4
              ♡ J 8
              ◇ A J 4 3
              ♣ 7 6 3

PARTNER                                    YOU
   ?                                       ♠ J 5 3 2
                                           ♡ 7 2
                                           ◇ K 9 7
                                           ♣ K J 5 3

              DECLARER
                 ?

The bidding:

| SOUTH | WEST | NORTH | EAST |
|-------|------|-------|------|
| 4 ♡ | Pass | Pass | Pass |

Against four hearts, your partner leads the spade king.
Which spade do you play?

**3.**

              DUMMY
              ♠ Q 10 5 2
              ♡ K 7 4
              ◇ A Q
              ♣ K J 10 3

PARTNER                                    YOU
   ?                                       ♠ 8 3
                                           ♡ Q J 10
                                           ◇ K J 8 7 5 3
                                           ♣ 8 5

              DECLARER
                 ?

The bidding:

| NORTH | EAST | SOUTH | WEST |
|-------|------|-------|------|
| 1 ♣ | Pass | 1 ♡ | Pass |
| 2 ♡ | Pass | 4 ♡ | Pass |
| Pass | Pass | | |

Against four hearts, partner leads the king of spades. Which spade do you play?

4.

DUMMY
♠ Q J 5 3
♡ A 9 8 4 2
◇ 8 5
♣ 8 4

YOU                                                    PARTNER
♠ A K 7 2                                                ?
♡ 6
◇ 9 7 6 2
♣ A J 10 2

DECLARER
?

The bidding:

| SOUTH | WEST | NORTH | EAST |
|-------|------|-------|------|
| 1 ♡ | Double | 3 ♡ | Pass |
| Pass | Pass | | |

Against three hearts, you lead the spade king on which partner drops the nine. You continue with the spade ace and partner plays the four. What card do you lead next?

5.

DUMMY
- ♠ K 9 4
- ♡ 8
- ◇ Q 6 4 2
- ♣ A K Q 10 4

YOU                                              PARTNER
- ♠ 7                                             ?
- ♡ A K 9 7 5 4
- ◇ 9 8
- ♣ 9 8 6 2

DECLARER
?

The bidding (North-South vulnerable):

| WEST | NORTH | EAST | SOUTH |
|------|-------|------|-------|
| 2 ♡ | Double | 4 ♡ | 6 ♠ |
| Pass | Pass | Pass | |

Playing weak two-bids, you deal and open two hearts.
North doubles for take-out, your partner raises to four
hearts, and South jumps to six spades. You lead the king
of hearts, on which partner plays the jack and declarer
plays the six. What do you play next?

**Answers to Quiz**

1. The diamond seven (or the six or five), *not* the two.
   When declarer leads a suit, it's correct to give the
   count. On this hand you should echo (play high-low)
   so that your partner will know you were dealt an even
   number of diamonds. (The seven is slightly superior
   to the six or the five because partner will be able to
   read it more easily.)
2. The spade two. When partner leads a suit, the come-on
   signal applies. You don't want spades continued so you
   should play your lowest card.
3. The spade three. You don't want your partner to
   continue spades and give you a ruff because you have

a natural trump trick anyway. You really want partner to switch to a diamond, because you plan to beat this contract with the diamond king, one trump trick, and two spade tricks. Unless partner shifts to a diamond right now, you may never get your diamond king. Unfortunately, there's no signal that can give two messages at once, such as, "Don't lead another spade, partner, please shift to diamonds." The best you can do is to play the spade three which means, "Don't continue spades, partner." From the appearance of dummy, partner will know that a diamond lead is called for.

4. The spade two. Partner is obviously going to ruff this round, and you should lead the two rather than the seven to indicate that you prefer him to return a club, the lower ranking of the two other suits.

5. The heart ace. Don't be alarmed by the singleton heart in dummy. Partner has asked you to continue hearts, and there is no reason to override his wishes. The actual hand may be

```
                    NORTH
                 ♠ K 9 4
                 ♡ 8
                 ◇ Q 6 4 2
                 ♣ A K Q 10 4

    WEST                          EAST
 ♠ 7                           ♠ J 8 6 3
 ♡ A K 9 7 5 4                 ♡ J 10 3 2
 ◇ 9 8                         ◇ K 10 7 5
 ♣ 9 8 6 2                     ♣ 3

                    SOUTH
                 ♠ A Q 10 5 2
                 ♡ Q 6
                 ◇ A J 3
                 ♣ J 7 5
```

Notice that if you lead another heart at trick two, dummy is forced to ruff. Now declarer will not find out about the bad trump break in time to finesse against your partner's jack and the slam will probably be defeated. If you lead another suit at trick two, South will easily make his contract.

# 14

# Two Tough Nuts to Crack

This chapter will explore and attempt to simplify two areas of bridge that are generally considered very complicated. These are the *probabilities of distribution* and the theory of *restricted choice*. You can play an excellent game of bridge without understanding either of them, but you'll never quite *feel* like an expert. A working acquaintance with these two areas, however, will not only increase your chances of making certain contracts, it will also cause you to appear superior in the eyes of your fellow players.

When we talk about the probabilities of distribution, we get into the field of mathematics and many people immediately become gun-shy. Don't let it bother you. To be a top-flight player, almost all you need to know about mathematics is how to count up to thirteen. Any more advanced calculation has already been worked out for you by the mathematicians. Good players become familiar with these play combinations, because even for a mathematician it would be far too tedious to work everything out at the table. As a matter of fact, mathematicians have no special advantage at the table and sometimes make very poor players. (As a class, lawyers have been found to make the best bridge players, probably because they have been trained in straightforward and logical thought.)

Where the mathematician really shines is at the party after the game. Here he can always impress his fellow bridge addicts with solutions to various percentage problems. Take the problem of the two red kings, for example:

Problem 1.

NORTH
♠ 6 4
♡ A Q J 6
♢ A Q J 4
♣ K 5 3

WEST          EAST
?             ?

SOUTH
♠ A K 8 2
♡ 10 9 3
♢ 10 9 2
♣ A Q J

You are South and find yourself in a contract of six no-trump. Before a card has been touched, what are your chances of making the slam? Obviously the only way to play the hand is to take repeated finesses in hearts and diamonds. You won't be defeated unless East holds both red kings.

What are the chances? Most good bridge players will say 75 percent. After all, East will have the heart king half the time. And half the time he has the heart king he will also have the diamond king. Half of a half is a quarter. So you will lose one quarter or 25 percent of the time, and make your slam 75 percent of the time.

This is only approximately correct. As the mathematician is happy to inform you, the exact chance of success is 76 percent.

You want him to explain this? First he gets out paper and pencil and puts a most intelligent expression on his face. Then he proceeds to write out a mathematical formula that somehow reminds you of Einstein's theory of relativity. By this time you are quite sorry you asked and are thoroughly bored by the whole subject.

Don't blame the mathematician too severely. He is a

victim of the system he was taught, whereby an extremely simple problem is handled as abstrusely as an advanced calculus equation.

Actually the problem is so simple that a ten-year-old should be able to solve it easily without paper or pencil and enjoy doing it *provided that it is explained to him visually.*

By the way, if you have no sense of humor and prefer to deal with life ponderously and profoundly, I suggest you skip the rest of this chapter. If you're still with me, however, I think you'll agree that this type of problem can be fun. So, erase that worried look and let's go!

First, imagine a round wooden tray with twenty-six holes in it. Now mentally draw a line down the center of the tray so that there are thirteen holes on the left side of the line and thirteen on the right. Assume that the tray is so constructed that a marble falling onto it will eventually

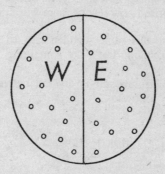

come to rest in one of the holes. No, it can't roll off the tray because there's a railing around the edge. And, by the way, the holes are laid out so that a marble has an equal chance of coming to rest in any one of them.

All right, now let's get two imaginary red marbles to represent the two red kings. Yes, the thirteen holes on the left of the line represent West's thirteen cards, while the thirteen holes on the right represent East's. The act of dropping the marbles represents the fate of the deal. (The other twenty-four cards in the East-West hands are immaterial to this problem.)

Now we're ready to drop the first marble. What are the chances of East getting it?

East has thirteen holes and there are twenty-six holes all together so East's chances are thirteen out of twenty-six or *one half*. Now, suppose East gets the first marble. What are his chances of also getting the second?

There are only twelve holes remaining on the East side because one is filled up by the first marble. And there are only twenty-five holes left on the entire tray, so East's chances of getting the second marble are twelve out of twenty-five. (Expressed as a fraction this is twelve twenty-fifths or $^{12}\!/_{25}$.) His chance of getting the first marble was one-half. His chance of getting the second is $^{12}\!/_{25}$. Therefore his chance of getting *both* is one half of $^{12}\!/_{25}$, which is $^{6}\!/_{25}$, or 24 percent. So you will be defeated 24 percent of the time, and you will make your slam 76 percent of the time. Give this problem to your bridge expert friends. You'll be surprised how few of them will know the answer.

You can use this same wooden tray to figure out any distribution problem. Let's try something a little harder this time.

Suppose the trump suit is divided between your hand and dummy as follows:

Problem 2.

NORTH (DUMMY)<br>
9 8 7 6

| WEST | | EAST |
|------|--|------|
| ? | | ? |

SOUTH (YOU)<br>
A K 10 5 4

Before any card has been played, what are the chances that West will have the doubleton queen-jack of trumps?

Get out the wooden tray and four marbles this time to

represent the four missing trumps, queen, jack, three, and two. Now let's have a look.

We'll drop the queen first, although it makes no difference what order is used. Her chances of going to West are thirteen out of twenty-six or $^{13}\!/_{26}$. Now the jack. His chances of going to West are $^{12}\!/_{25}$. Next drop the three. Remember, if West is going to get the queen-jack alone, the three and the two must go to East. East's chances of getting the three are $^{13}\!/_{24}$, since there are thirteen holes still open in the East hand and only twenty-four holes open on the entire tray. And finally East's chances of getting the two are $^{12}\!/_{23}$. So the chances that West will have the queen-jack of trumps and East the three-two are

$$\frac{13}{26} \times \frac{12}{25} \times \frac{13}{24} \times \frac{12}{23}$$

which comes to about 6.78 percent.

Because we used four marbles this time there was more multiplication involved. And unfortunately, the multiplication gets more tedious the more marbles we use.

Now that you know how to figure the chances of any particular distribution occurring, here is a handy table of the more common distributions to save you the trouble:

DISTRIBUTION OF CARDS IN THE TWO UNKNOWN HANDS

| Cards Outstanding in a Suit | Division | Percent Probability |
|---|---|---|
| 2 | 1–1 | 52.00 |
|   | 2–0 | 48.00 |
| 3 | 2–1 | 78.00 |
|   | 3–0 | 22.00 |
| 4 | 3–1 | 49.74 |
|   | 2–2 | 40.70 |
|   | 4–0 | 9.57 |

| Cards Outstanding in a Suit | Division | Percent Probability |
|:---:|:---:|:---:|
| 5 | 3–2 | 67.83 |
|   | 4–1 | 28.26 |
|   | 5–0 | 3.91 |
| 6 | 4–2 | 48.45 |
|   | 3–3 | 35.53 |
|   | 5–1 | 14.53 |
|   | 6–0 | 1.49 |
| 7 | 4–3 | 62.17 |
|   | 5–2 | 30.52 |
|   | 6–1 | 6.78 |
|   | 7–0 | 0.52 |
| 8 | 5–3 | 47.12 |
|   | 4–4 | 32.72 |
|   | 6–2 | 17.14 |
|   | 7–1 | 2.86 |
|   | 8–0 | 0.16 |

(Do not try to memorize this table. Do notice, however, that an odd number of cards tends to break as evenly as possible but an even number of cards does not. Thus if you are missing five spades you can expect them to break three-two. But if you are missing six spades they probably will not break three-three.)

Instead of using the wooden tray for Problem 2, for example, we could simply have checked the 2–2 division in the table, where we find that four cards will produce a 2–2 split 40.70 percent of the time. As there are six possible doubletons that West could hold (queen-jack, queen-three, queen-two, jack-three, jack-two, and three-two) the chances that he will hold any particular doubleton are one sixth of 40.70 percent, or 6.78 percent of the time.

One question I am frequently asked is, "What are my chances of holding thirteen spades?" Even this could be worked out on the wooden tray. Simply add twenty-six more holes for the North and South cards and the chances of getting all thirteen spades are

$$\frac{13}{52} \times \frac{12}{51} \times \frac{11}{50} \times \frac{10}{49} \times \frac{9}{48} \times \frac{8}{47} \times \frac{7}{46} \times \frac{6}{45} \times$$

$$\frac{5}{44} \times \frac{4}{43} \times \frac{3}{42} \times \frac{2}{41} \times \frac{1}{40}$$

We need a machine to multiply this one. The answer is you will hold thirteen spades once in every 635,013,559,600 deals!

Infinitely more remote are the chances of all four players each holding a thirteen-card suit. This occurs once in every 2,235,197,406,895,366,368,301,560,000 deals. It's difficult to even begin to comprehend such a number. Imagine that the entire population of the world were to sit down and play bridge continuously day and night, 365 days a year, year after year without stopping. Once in about every 100,000,000,000,000 years someone would deal this perfect hand.

This is why experts put so little faith in the newspaper reports every year or so that someone dealt a perfect hand. Where do these reports come from? Let me tell you a true story.

Many years ago a friend of mine was strolling along the deck of a ship when he saw four passengers playing bridge. As he passed the table he calmly picked up the spare deck of cards and carried it to the rail where he quickly sorted it. He then replaced the cards, still unobserved by the players, and mingled with the other passengers at the far end of the deck to await developments.

The outcry was not long in coming and the excitement was tremendous. The story hit all the newspapers. And the four players, well-respected members of society, all swore that no one had tampered with the cards!

## The Theory of Restricted Choice

One of the least-understood concepts in bridge is what is called the theory of restricted choice. Let's look again at Problem 2:

NORTH (DUMMY)
9 8 7 6

SOUTH (YOU)
A K 10 5 4

Assume that you lead the ace on which West drops the jack. Is this more likely to be a singleton or is it more likely that West holds the queen-jack doubleton? If it is a singleton, you should go to dummy and take a second-round finesse. And, if it's from the queen-jack doubleton you should just lay down the king.

As we determined earlier, when the queen, jack, three, and two are missing, West can be expected to hold the queen-jack alone 6.78 percent of the time.

To discover the probability of West holding the single-ton jack and East the queen, three, and two, we can drop four more marbles, but as we have a table handy it's easier to look up the 3–1 distribution. When four cards are missing, a 3–1 distribution will occur 49.74 percent of the time. In one half these cases, East will hold the singleton, and in the other half it will be with West. In other words, West will hold a singleton 24.87 percent of the time. As there are four possible singletons (queen, jack, three, or two), any particular singleton will occur in only one quarter of these cases. Thus the chance that West will be dealt the singleton jack is 6.22 percent. (Check this with the marbles if you wish.)

As the probability that West will hold the doubleton queen-jack is 6.78 percent and the probability that he will hold any particular singleton is 6.22 percent, it may appear that the slightly better play is to lead out the ace and king.

This is not the right answer, however. In fact the second-round finesse is almost twice as good. Why? The answer to this and many related problems lies in the theory of restricted choice.

The reasoning behind restricted choice is this. If West held the doubleton queen-jack he would play either card at random because he knows they are equals. About half of the time he could be expected to play the queen and half of the time the jack. He would play the jack from the queen-jack doubleton half of 6.78 percent, or 3.39 percent, of the time. With the singleton jack, however, he has no choice and must play the jack all 6.22 percent of the time. Thus the second-round finesse is almost twice as good a play.

If this explanation is not entirely clear, let's try using a can of paint.

Remember, in this problem the queen and jack are equal. So imagine that before any cards are played declarer voluntarily closes his eyes and an impartial observer removes the queen and jack from wherever they are in the opponents' hands, and paints the faces of both cards so no one can tell them apart. For convenience we will have him put an identical H (for honor) in the corner of each. Then he replaces the cards as they were in the East-West hands. Declarer opens his eyes and leads the ace on which West drops an H.

Does West hold the doubleton HH, which as we have seen occurs 6.78 percent of the time? Or does he hold a singleton H? Remember that any particular singleton occurs 6.22 percent of the time. There are now two singleton H's that West could hold, so the 6.22 percent becomes 12.44 percent. Thus the chances that the card played on the ace was a singleton H are almost twice that of its being from the doubleton HH. Obviously the second-round finesse is the right play.

In real life there is no impartial observer to paint the cards for us. But the second-round finesse is still almost twice as good a play.

If you have followed this chapter you have grasped two of what are generally considered the most difficult concepts in bridge. Thanks to a wooden tray, some marbles, and a can of paint.

# 15

## Tips for Experts Only

This chapter is intended for expert or very near expert players *only*. If you are not in this category, I suggest that you skip this material, since it may confuse you. The suggestions and theories presented here are not standard. In fact most of them have not been published before.

### What to Do When Opponents Interfere with Blackwood

Consider the following hand (North-South are vulnerable):

```
                          NORTH
                       ♠ Q 10 5 4
                       ♡ A 4 3
                       ◇ 6 4 2
                       ♣ 9 8 6

        WEST                              EAST
     ♠ —                              ♠ 7 6 2
     ♡ K J 10 7 6 5                   ♡ Q 9 8
     ◇ 5                              ◇ J 8 7 3
     ♣ K 7 5 4 3 2                    ♣ Q J 10

                          SOUTH
                       ♠ A K J 9 8 3
                       ♡ 2
                       ◇ A K Q 10 9
                       ♣ A
```

The bidding has gone:

| SOUTH | WEST | NORTH | EAST |
|-------|------|-------|------|
| 2 ♠   | 3 ♡  | 3 ♠   | 4 ♡  |
| 4 NT  | 7 ♡  | Pass  | Pass |
| ?     |      |       |      |

Suppose you are South in this hand. You are well on your way to a vulnerable grand slam when West throws a spanner into your "Blackwoods" with a premature sacrifice. Do you double for a paltry 500-point set, or do you gamble on making a score of 2210 and bid seven spades?

There are several arrangements that a pair can make to cover the case when an opponent interferes with Blackwood. The trouble is that the situation comes up so infrequently you are apt to forget what arrangements you made when you're actually faced with the problem.

The method I have arranged to use with regular partners has the advantage of being so simple and logical that once you hear it you can hardly forget it. It is based on two logical premises. First, it assumes that the Blackwood bidder is captain and must be in complete charge of placing the final contract. Second, it assumes that the Blackwood bidder should be able to judge, from the previous bidding, within one ace of how many aces his partner holds.

When an opponent interferes with Blackwood, responder should alternately double or pass as follows:

> *With no aces*, double.
> *With one ace*, pass.
> *With two aces*, double.
> *With three aces*, pass.
> *With four aces*, double.

It's easy to remember that the double signifies no aces because logically if you have no aces you are least interested in proceeding with the slam effort. Therefore you're most inclined to double the opponents in such a situation.

In the above hand, North should pass over West's seven-heart bid to indicate *one* ace. South can now bid the grand slam with complete confidence.

Shortly after the first edition of this book appeared I inspected the convention card of a woman opponent and was puzzled by the notation "DOPI." My request for an explanation led to raised eyebrows. "It's your convention," I was told. "Over Blackwood, double zero, pass one." So it has been "DOPI," pronounced Dopey, ever since.

## Blackwood and the Grand Slam Force Combined

Consider the following hand. You are South and are holding ♠ A 10 8 7 3   ♡ K Q J 5 4   ◇ A   ♣ K 4. The bidding has gone

| SOUTH | NORTH |
|-------|-------|
| 1 ♠ | 3 ♠ |
| 4 NT | 5 ♡ |
| ? | |

At this point you know the hand belongs in seven spades if partner holds the king and queen of that suit. Unfortunately you couldn't use the grand slam force earlier because you didn't know about his two aces. And it's too

209

late to bid five no-trump now, because partner will think you are asking for kings.

To cover this situation, I recommend using six clubs as a type of grand slam force. As partner already knows about the ace of trumps, it asks only about the king and queen of trumps. Responder bids a grand slam with both these cards.

In the above example South would bid six clubs and North would jump to seven spades with the king and the queen.


## An Inferential Take-out Double

There are many bids that come under the heading of "inferential." A well-known example is the case where both opponents announce length in a suit in which you have three small cards. Any bid by you at this point is probably based on the "inference" that partner is very short in this suit.

An inferential take-out double, however, is relatively unknown. Consider the following situation:

| WEST | NORTH | EAST | SOUTH |
|------|-------|------|-------|
| 1 NT | Pass | 2 ◇ | ? |
| | | (or 2 ♡ or 2 ♠) | |

Provided East's bid shows weakness, South may double for take-out with a singleton or void in East's suit almost regardless of the number of points in his hand.

Hand A: ♠ A 5 4 2   ♡ K J 9 7   ◇ 6   ♣ K J 10 9

Hand B: ♠ A 5 4 2   ♡ J 10 6 5   ◇ 6   ♣ J 10 8 7

Most good players would double automatically with Hand A and would pass automatically with Hand B. In a high-level game, it is correct to double with *both* hands. In fact Hand B is likely to turn out to be a better double than Hand A.

The reasoning is this. On the bidding, East-West can be expected to hold an average of about 21 points and a built-in diamond fit. This means that North-South probably hold about 19 points and a very probable fit in one of the other three suits. With Hand B, South has the advantage of knowing that most of his side's strength lies *over* the no-trump bidder. The entire layout could be

NORTH
♠ 8 7
♡ K 9 8 4
♢ K 9 4 2
♣ A Q 9

<table>
<tr><td>

WEST
♠ K J 9 6
♡ A Q 3
♢ A 7
♣ K 6 5 3

</td><td>

EAST
♠ Q 10 3
♡ 7 2
♢ Q J 10 8 5 3
♣ 4 2

</td></tr>
</table>

SOUTH
♠ A 5 4 2
♡ J 10 6 5
♢ 6
♣ J 10 8 7

Notice that if South fails to double, his side will get shut out of the auction. North's length in diamonds will prevent him from competing, and East-West will probably score a partial. If South doubles, however, North will bid two hearts and North-South will get the plus score.

## The Cooperative Slam Double

Consider the following auction:

| SOUTH | WEST | NORTH | EAST |
|-------|--------|-------|------|
| 4 ♠ | Double | Pass | 5 ♡ |
| Pass | Pass | 5 ♠ | 6 ♡ |
| Pass | Pass | ? | |

If East-West can make six hearts, North-South obviously have a profitable sacrifice. On the other hand if North-South have two defensive tricks between them, they certainly don't want to take a phantom save.

How can North-South be sure whether or not they have two defensive tricks? The answer is by some form of cooperative slam double.

Until recently I never used any form of cooperative slam double. The hand which converted me occurred in the 1964 Trials for the International Team:

```
                BECKER
              ♠ A 7
              ♡ —
              ◊ Q 9 7 4 3 2
              ♣ K 8 5 4 2

  H. PORTUGAL                   M. PORTUGAL
♠ Q J                        ♠ 2
♡ K Q J 10 6                 ♡ A 9 7 5 4 3 2
◊ A J 8 6                    ◊ 5
♣ 9 7                        ♣ A Q 10 6

                HAYDEN
              ♠ K 10 9 8 6 5 4 3
              ♡ 8
              ◊ K 10
              ♣ J 3
```

Only East and West were vulnerable and the bidding went as shown above. When East's six-heart bid came around to North, he made a penalty double and I passed. East made six hearts doubled, and obviously a sacrifice at six spades on our part would have been profitable.

Now that the horse had been stolen, we figured out a way to lock the stable door.

The following method of using the cooperative slam double in competitive auctions varies slightly from other methods in use. I believe it is the most sensible and the most accurate.

It is based on the logical agreement that if the player

*in the last seat* expects to set the contract (i.e., he has two *defensive* tricks), he should *pass* to be sure of playing it there. If he expects the opponents to make their contract (i.e., has no *defensive* tricks) he should sacrifice. And if he is not certain whether or not they can make it (i.e., he has about one *defensive* trick) he should double. Partner will leave in the double with one *defensive* trick and take the sacrifice himself with no *defensive* tricks.

As a corollary, the player *in the first seat* should double immediately with two *defensive* tricks to keep his partner from sacrificing. With one or no *defensive* tricks, he should pass.

In a nutshell:

> *In first seat*, double with two tricks and pass with one or no tricks.

> *In last seat*, pass with two tricks, double with one trick, and sacrifice with no tricks.

If we had been playing cooperative doubles in the trials, North's double would have meant that he was uncertain of defeating the slam. Having minimum values for my previous bidding, I would have removed the double to six spades. This would have gone down 500 or 700 points, a very good score compared with that of a vulnerable slam against us.

Obviously the cooperative slam double is primarily valuable for International Match Point or total point scoring, where slam decisions are so vital. The match-point or board-a-match player will find it a relatively unprofitable refinement.

### The Delayed Unusual No-Trump

Every expert is a specialist in the art of reopening a dead auction. A well-known maneuver in a high-level game is the delayed take-out double. Consider the following hand: As West you hold ♠ 7 ♡ A Q 10 8 6 2 ◇ K J 10 ♣ K J 3.

213

The bidding has gone

| SOUTH | WEST | NORTH | EAST |
|-------|------|-------|------|
| 1 ♠ | 2 ♡ | 2 ♠ | Pass |
| Pass | ? | | |

No red-blooded West can be expected to sell out for two spades with this hand. The most flexible action at this point is to double. This allows partner to bid diamonds or clubs, but it naturally suggests a strong preference for hearts.

A relatively unknown maneuver, however, although just as logical, is the delayed unusual no-trump.

Example:
As West you hold    ♠ 7    ♡ J 8    ◇ A Q 10 2
♣ A K J 9 4 3.

The bidding:

| SOUTH | WEST | NORTH | EAST |
|-------|------|-------|------|
| 1 ♠ | 2 ♣ | 2 ♠ | Pass |
| Pass | ? | | |

West might bid three clubs at this point. A more flexible bid, however, is two no-trump, the delayed unusual no-trump. (West can hardly want to play no-trump on this auction.) The unusual no-trump shows interest in both minor suits but naturally suggests a strong preference for clubs.


## Negative Responses to the Grand Slam Force

Consider the following bidding:

| SOUTH | NORTH |
|-------|-------|
| 1 ♡ | 3 ♡ |
| 5 NT | ? |

With two of the top three honors in hearts, it is standard for North to bid seven hearts. But what does he bid when he doesn't have two of the three top honors? What do responses of six clubs, six diamonds, or six hearts mean? There's no standard answer to this. Any good pair has to work out its own meanings. Obviously it would be extravagant to use all three bids to deliver this same message: "I don't have two of the top three honors, partner."

The prime considerations in assigning a meaning in this kind of a situation are *logic* and *simplicity*. Remember, the occasion to use the bid probably won't come up until six months after you assign a meaning to it. If the meaning is logical and simple, it will pop into your mind readily. If it is illogical or complicated, either you or your partner will forget it.

The meaning I prefer to use is based on the general rule, "The more you have, the more you bid."

Thus in the above example, North would bid six clubs with the worst possible trump holding, considering his previous bidding. He'd bid six diamonds holding the trumps one would expect from the auction. He'd bid six hearts with any maximum trump support, which does *not* include two of the top three honors in trumps.

If partner has the appropriate trump holding, he may be able to bid the grand slam opposite a maximum response.

Obviously, the lower ranking the trump suit, the less room you have for refinements. If the trump suit happens to be clubs, the response to deny two of the top three honors must always be six clubs.

### Splinter Bids

In the early sixties I developed a convention which I described in the first edition of this book under the heading "The Unusual Jump to Show a Singleton." This proved so valuable that it is now used by a majority of the top tournament players in this country. It is now called the splinter bid, and this is how it works.

Any jump to a meaningless level in an unbid suit announces a fit with partner's suit, suggests a slam, and guarantees at most a singleton in the suit bid.

```
        WEST      EAST
        1 ◇       1 ♠
        4 ♣
```

If West really held clubs he would bid two clubs or three clubs depending on the strength of his hand. Four clubs is therefore an "idle bid," entirely meaningless in the absence of partnership agreement. So we agree that it means a spade fit, a very strong hand, and a singleton or a void in clubs. West might hold ♠ K J x x ♡ A J x ◇ A K J x x ♣ x.

The ability to locate a singleton becomes extremely valuable at the slam level.

Example 1.

```
        WEST              EAST
    ♠ A Q x x x x      ♠ K 10 x x
    ♡ x               ♡ A J x x
    ◇ K Q x           ◇ A 10 x x
    ♣ 10 x x          ♣ x
```

Using standard methods, the auction might go

```
        WEST              EAST
        1 ♠               3 ♠
        4 ♠               Pass
```

Playing the unusual jump to show a singleton, the bidding would go

```
        WEST              EAST
        1 ♠               4 ♣
        4 NT              5 ♡
        6 ♠               Pass
```

Here, four clubs is the equivalent of a strong three-spade raise which includes a singleton club. West is now able to check on aces and bid the slam. Naturally, a bid of four diamonds or four hearts would show the same three-spade raise with a singleton diamond or heart.

With a void, responder may proceed just as though he held a singleton. If he's given another chance to bid, however, he cue-bids the suit again showing that the singleton was really a void. Thus:

Example 2.

|  | WEST |  | EAST |
|---|---|---|---|
| ♠ | A Q J x x x | ♠ | K 10 x x x |
| ♡ | A K Q x | ♡ | J 9 x x |
| ◇ | — | ◇ | K Q J x |
| ♣ | J x x | ♣ | — |

The bidding:

| WEST | EAST |
|---|---|
| 1 ♠ | 4 ♣ |
| 4 ♡ | 5 ♣ |
| 7 ♠ | |

If Blackwood is used as in Example 1, the void will show up automatically. Suppose East in Example 1 held ♠ K 10 x x   ♡ A 9 x x   ◇ A 9 x x x   ♣ —. The bidding would now go

| WEST | EAST |
|---|---|
| 1 ♠ | 4 ♣ |
| 4 NT | 6 ♡ |
| 7 ♠ | |

Note that in answer to Blackwood East bids six hearts instead of five hearts. This shows two aces and a void. West can now confidently bid the grand slam.

The splinter bid works well in this sequence:

| WEST | EAST |
|---|---|
| 1 ◇ | 1 ♡ |
| 3 ♠ | |

217

This shows a four-heart raise with a singleton spade.

Notice that auctions like

| WEST | EAST |
|------|------|
| 1 ♡ | 3 ♡ |

or

| WEST | EAST |
|------|------|
| 1 ♣ | 1 ♡ |
| 4 ♡ | |

tend to deny possession of a singleton. By the way, the sequence

| WEST | NORTH | EAST |
|------|-------|------|
| 1 ♡ | 1 ♠ | 3 ♠ |

must show specifically a singleton spade. With a void, it would be more logical for East to bid two spades, not three spades.

The chief value of the unusual jump, of course, is to get you to slam when one partner has a singleton opposite his partner's worthless suit. An additional, and very substantial benefit, however, is to keep you *out* of slams when one player has a singleton opposite his partner's strength.

Example:

| WEST | EAST |
|------|------|
| ♠ A Q x x x | ♠ K J 10 x x |
| ♡ A | ♡ K x x |
| ◇ K Q x | ◇ x |
| ♣ J x x x | ♣ A x x x |

Using standard methods, it is very difficult for any good pair to stop at four spades on these cards. Playing singleton-showing bids, however, the auction would go

| WEST | EAST |
|------|------|
| 1 ♠ | 4 ◇ |
| 4 ♠ | |

When East shows a singleton diamond, West mentally tears up his diamond king-queen. His enthusiasm now sufficiently dampened, he is able to put on the brakes. Notice that even five spades is in jeopardy on these cards. Of course, if East's minor-suit holdings were reversed he would respond four clubs and West would easily get to slam.

Many players extend splinter bids to situations that arise after a minor-suit opening.

| WEST | EAST |
|------|------|
| 1 ♣ | 3 ♠ |

East is showing a forcing raise in clubs (usually five-card support or better) and a singleton or void spade. He denies a four-card heart suit, since he would then have preferred to show the suit in the hope of finding a major-suit fit. He might hold ♠ x ♡ A x x ◇ K 10 x x ♣ A Q x x x.

If West has no wasted values in spades he may be able to reach a good six-club contract. And if he does have considerable spade strength, he can bid three no-trump, slowing down East and probably ending the bidding.

This means of course that if West has ♠ K J 9 x x x x ♡ x x ◇ x x x ♣ x he can no longer make the preemptive response of three spades. But preempting one's partner in this fashion is a procedure of doubtful merit and one spade is an entirely satisfactory response with such a hand.

Finally, be careful about this sequence:

| WEST | EAST |
|------|------|
| 1 ♠ | 4 ♡ |

This is a desirable splinter bid, but it *sounds* natural. Do not use it unless you are sure you and your partner will be on the same wavelength.

# 16

# Bridge Tales

When bridge players get together they entertain one another with stories about hands. In the belief that every book should have some entertainment value, this chapter is devoted to amusing hands from real life.

The best hand I ever held, and also one of the most frustrating, occurred in a rubber bridge game at the New York Cavendish club. My partner was the late Harry Fishbein, famous major-domo of the Mayfair Club. Vulnerable against nonvulnerable opponents, I picked up the following incredible collection:

♠ A K Q J x x    ♡ —    ◊ A K Q 10 x x x    ♣ —

It's hard to imagine that anything tragic could happen to this beauty, isn't it?

By the way, we don't just play for peanuts in this game and even if we did, a vulnerable grand slam comes to a heck of a lot of peanuts!

Sam Stayman, on my right, dealt and opened three hearts. Now if I had had an average partner I would have just picked a suit and bid a grand slam myself. With an expert for a partner, however, I knew I could find out which suit was better, so I bid four hearts. My left-hand opponent passed, Fishy jumped to six clubs, and Stayman passed. This development didn't worry me. (After all, I held the spade suit and I could always bid seven spades if the bidding got out of control.) So I bid six hearts to force Fishy to choose another suit. Do you see any danger in this, playing with an expert? I didn't. In fact I was mentally patting myself on the back for handling the situation so adroitly when catastrophe struck. Over six hearts Fishy inadvertently bid six diamonds!

Of course the opponents kindly pointed out that six diamonds was insufficient. Under the laws Fishy could either make the bid sufficient in the same suit by bidding seven diamonds in which case there is no penalty, or he could substitute any other sufficient call, in which case his *partner would be barred from the bidding.*

Fishy naturally hated to bid seven diamonds. (He had only a small doubleton.) So he corrected the bid to six no-trump and I was barred from the auction with the best hand I had ever seen!

It seems funny now, but imagine how I felt having to lay that hand down as dummy at six no-trump.

As an anticlimax Fishy actually held ♠ x x ♡ A x x x ◊ x x ♣ K J x x x. Both my suits broke and he easily made six no-trump but, of course, either seven spades or seven diamonds was laydown.

*         *         *

In contrast, here is an example of a terrible hand that turned out to be lucky. Playing in the National Women's pairs with Sylvia Stein of Detroit, I was South, neither side was vulnerable, and I found myself looking at this gem:

♠ 742   ♡ 654   ◊ 6532   ♣ 432

Sylvia dealt and bid two clubs (a game force but not necessarily showing a club suit). East passed and I responded two diamonds (negative). West overcalled two spades and the bidding went pass, pass, back to me. What should I do next?

| NORTH | EAST | SOUTH | WEST |
|-------|------|-------|------|
| (SYLVIA) | | (ME) | |
| 2 ♣ | Pass | 2 ◇ | 2 ♠ |
| Pass | Pass | ? | |

Interesting problem, isn't it? I obviously couldn't pass when Sylvia had opened the bidding with two clubs. But what would be the weakest bid I could make at this point? I finally decided to double, which turned out to be right. The complete deal was

NORTH
♠ 8 3
♡ A K Q
◇ A K 9
♣ A K J 8 7

WEST
♠ A K Q J 10
♡ 10 8 7 3
◇ 10 4
♣ 9 6

EAST
♠ 9 6 5
♡ J 9 2
◇ Q J 8 7
♣ Q 10 5

SOUTH
♠ 7 4 2
♡ 6 5 4
◇ 6 5 3 2
♣ 4 3 2

Two spades doubled went for 300, which gave us a top because North-South had no game. Notice that Sylvia had made an excellent pass over two spades. Most players would automatically have taken action over two spades.

\*        \*        \*

Neither vulnerable:

```
                    NORTH
                   (HAYDEN)
                  ♠ Q 8
                  ♡ 10 6 3
                  ◊ A Q J 9 6
                  ♣ A Q 4

   WEST                              EAST
  (STAYMAN)                        (MITCHELL)
 ♠ 5 4 3                          ♠ J 10 7 2
 ♡ A 8 5                          ♡ K Q 7 4
 ◊ K 5 3 2                        ◊ 10 8 7
 ♣ 10 5 2                         ♣ 7 6

                    SOUTH
                   (BECKER)
                  ♠ A K 9 6
                  ♡ J 9 2
                  ◊ 4
                  ♣ K J 9 8 3
```

The bidding:

| SOUTH | WEST | NORTH | EAST |
|-------|------|-------|------|
| 1 ♣ | Pass | 1 ◊ | Pass |
| 1 ♠ | Pass | 3 ♣ | Pass |
| 4 ♣ | Pass | 4 ♠ | Pass |
| 6 ♣ | Pass | Pass | Pass |

Here is a sensational hand from the 1963 International Team Trials in Miami. B. Jay Becker and I were playing against Sam Stayman and Victor Mitchell. For some obscure reason we had decided to use Gerber over minor suits as well as no-trump. When Becker bid four clubs however, he had forgotten all about our ridiculous agreement. Unfortunately I remembered it and bid four spades to show two aces. Assuming my four-spade bid was natural, Becker read me for a singleton heart. (A person who bids two suits and jumps in a third suit is supposed to have at most a singleton in the fourth suit.) He happily leaped to six clubs.

Now Stayman had also heard this strong bidding and "knew" that I was very short in hearts, so he decided to attack with a diamond lead. Believe it or not the hand could no longer be defeated thanks to my *six* of hearts! Interchange my six with Stayman's five and the contract can't be made.

Although my dummy must have horrified Becker he maintained his usual poker face and calmly finessed the diamond jack at trick one. He then cashed the diamond ace throwing a heart and ruffed a diamond. He led a trump to the ace and ruffed another diamond establishing dummy's queen. He now cashed the club king and queen ending in the dummy with this the position:

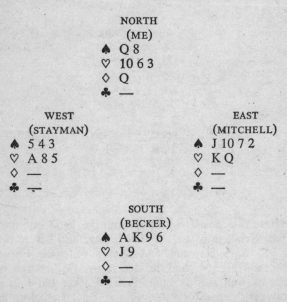

NORTH
(ME)
♠ Q 8
♡ 10 6 3
♢ Q
♣ —

WEST
(STAYMAN)
♠ 5 4 3
♡ A 8 5
♢ —
♣ —

EAST
(MITCHELL)
♠ J 10 7 2
♡ K Q
♢ —
♣ —

SOUTH
(BECKER)
♠ A K 9 6
♡ J 9
♢ —
♣ —

He now led the good diamond queen, on which East had to throw a heart honor. South threw the heart nine and Stayman parted with a spade. Becker next cashed the spade queen and led a spade. Mitchell played the ten and South won with the king and led his heart jack! The defenders were through! If West ducked, East would win and have to lead a spade away from his jack-seven into declarer's ace-nine. And if West rose with the heart ace he would have to lead away from his eight-five of hearts into my ten-six. The defenders were in a state of semi-shock by the end of the hand and you can't blame them. Mitchell kept muttering, "He couldn't have done it without the six of hearts."

Becker answered solemnly, "We naturally wouldn't have bid so much without the six of hearts"!

\* \* \*

One of the silliest mistakes I ever made occurred on this hand from the 1964 Nationals in Portland, Oregon.

```
                    NORTH
                 ♠ 8 6
                 ♡ A 4 2
                 ◇ Q 5 3
                 ♣ K 10 9 6 3

    WEST                            EAST
 ♠ K Q J                         ♠ 5 4
 ♡ J 10 8 5                      ♡ 9 7 6
 ◇ 9 6 4                         ◇ 10 8 7
 ♣ A J 2                         ♣ Q 8 7 5 4

                    SOUTH
                 ♠ A 10 9 7 3 2
                 ♡ K Q 3
                 ◇ A K J 2
                 ♣ —
```

I was South, and when I picked up my hand the cards were already sorted for me. Unfortunately, three of the spades had been placed between the red suits and as I glanced at my hand I saw ♠ A 10 9  ♡ K Q 3 ♠ 7 3 2  ◇ A K J 2.

225

I bid one no-trump with this "balanced" hand. Partner raised me to two no-trump, and remembering my seventeen points I bid three no-trump without looking back at my cards. It wasn't until West had led the spade king and the dummy came down that I noticed I was a bit short in the club department. However I won the spade and returned a spade eventually making five no-trump, losing only two spade tricks. Our score of 460 was a top on the board, since the field was in four spades making five for a score of 450.

Imagine how annoyed West was to find he had lost his ace of clubs on this auction! Yes, I was embarrassed!

*       *       *

The next hand is a horrible disaster, which I shall never forget because of the lambasting I got from my partner. This happened in a national tournament many years ago. My partner was a very famous expert and I was practically unknown at the time. In spite of the fact that we had never played together before, things went well and going into the final session we found ourselves second in the field. We were seated North-South at Table One, and because my partner was one of the biggest names in bridge we had a large ring of kibitzers. On the very first board of the final session I made a terrible goof.

Neither vulnerable:

NORTH
♠ K 5 4
♡ K 2
◇ Q J 10 6 5
♣ A K 5

WEST
♠ Q J 8 6
♡ Q J 10 6
◇ A K 9
♣ 8 6

EAST
♠ A 10 3
♡ A 9 8 7
◇ 8 7 3 2
♣ Q 2

SOUTH
(ME)
♠ 9 7 2
♡ 5 4 3
◇ 4
♣ J 10 9 7 4 3

The bidding:

| WEST | NORTH | EAST | SOUTH |
|------|-------|------|-------|
| 1 ◇ | Double | Redouble | 2 ♣ |
| Pass | 3 ♣ | 3 ◇ | Pass |
| Pass | Double | Pass | 4 ♣ |
| Double | Pass | Pass | Pass |

When North doubled three diamonds I got cold feet and pulled it to four clubs, which went for 500. Instead of a top we obviously had a bottom. Partner was furious. "Young lady, I don't want you ever to take me out of a penalty double again as long as you live," etc. He went on ranting for several minutes. I held on tightly to the table and swore to myself that I wouldn't open my mouth. The worst part was to see the kibitzers beginning to feel so sorry for me under the tirade. What I felt like pointing out was that if he had only passed three diamonds we would have had a tremendous board. We had created a situation in the bidding where East-West had been talked out of their four-heart contract. Any North-South plus score was bound to be sensational. Naturally partner was even more irritated because subconsciously he knew the fault was half his. However I realized that if I pointed out an error to a famous expert like him in front of a ring of kibitzers all hope of ever recovering partnership harmony would be gone forever. I kept saying to myself, "What difference does it make if twenty kibitzers spend the rest of their lives thinking you are a tongue-tied half-wit? The important thing is to win and you can't win if you don't get your partner back into a good humor."

Finally the outburst subsided and we both picked up our cards for the second board in stony silence. This was hopeless so I put my cards down on the table.

I said, "Partner, I think you've got some more on your mind."

"As a matter of fact I do," and he went on for another minute or two.

When he ran out of words this time I said, "You know I hate to start this next board until you've got it all off your chest."

Finally he smiled. Everyone breathed a sigh of relief. Partnership harmony restored, we managed to avoid any other disasters and we went on to win the championship. If any of those twenty kibitzers ever reads this, I'm not really a helpless and tongue-tied female: It was all for the good of the cause.

\*　　　　\*　　　　\*

I am frequently asked if woman's intuition helps at the bridge table. I don't know the answer. Here's the type of good play that looks like intuition. (Besides I'm tired of writing about my mistakes.) See what you think.

North-South vulnerable:

```
                    NORTH
                    ♠ 8 6
                    ♡ K 10 8 6 5 2
                    ◇ 10 3
                    ♣ K Q 3

     WEST                            EAST
     ♠ K 3                           ♠ 10 9 7 6
     ♡ J                             ♡ Q 9 7 4
     ◇ A K J 8 7 5                   ◇ 4
     ♣ 9 6 5 2                       ♣ J 10 7 4

                    SOUTH
                    ♠ A Q J 4 2
                    ♡ A 3
                    ◇ Q 9 6 2
                    ♣ A 8
```

The bidding:

| SOUTH | WEST | NORTH | EAST |
|-------|------|-------|------|
| 1 ♠   | 3 ◇  | 3 ♡   | Pass |
| 3 NT  | Pass | Pass  | Pass |

I was South on this deal from the 1964 Spingold Championship. West led the diamond king and continued with the ace, on which East parted, somewhat reluctantly, with a small club. West switched to the heart jack, which I won with the ace. If the hearts broke I was in good shape, so I naturally continued with a heart to the king. When West showed out, I could no longer bring in the heart suit and I had to rely on the spades. I had two heart tricks and three club tricks and a diamond coming to me, so I needed three more tricks. How should I play the spades?

As the cards lie you can see I would be down if I made the normal play of a small spade to the queen. West would win and lead a club. East would eventually make a spade trick and cash the heart queen for the setting trick. (Of course I knew West had the spade king. He would hardly have tried to set up diamonds by cashing the top

229

honors if he hadn't had an entry.) But the same fate would befall me if I led a spade to the ace and continued with the spade queen.

So I led a spade to the ace and then led a *small* spade from my hand. West won his king and I took the rest of the tricks.

How did I know West had K x in spades and not K x x? Because of East's slight reluctance to part with a club at trick two. If East had held five clubs, he could have spared one painlessly. And if he only had four clubs, he had to have four spades, leaving his partner with the doubleton king.

\*        \*        \*

People often ask if being a mathematician helps me at the bridge table. The answer is, "Practically never." Here's a hand from the 1965 North America–Argentina match, which will show you what I mean.

NORTH
♠ J 8
♡ A K 6 5
♢ 6 5 2
♣ A Q 10 4

SOUTH
♠ A Q 9 7 6 5 3
♡ —
♢ K J 7
♣ K J 5

The bidding:

| SOUTH | WEST | NORTH | EAST |
|-------|------|-------|------|
| 1 ♠   | Pass | 2 ♣   | Pass |
| 3 ♠   | Pass | 6 ♠   | Pass |
| Pass  | Pass |       |      |

I was South. The Argentine player on my left opened the ace of diamonds against my six-spade contract and then he switched to a club. How should I play to avoid a trump loser?

Of course I had to assume that East had the spade king. There are now three plausible lines of attack.

1. I could lead the spade jack from dummy, and if East covered I could win with the ace and cash the spade queen. This wins if East has K 10, K 4, K 2, or K 4 2 of spades. (This adds up to about a 26½ percent chance of success.)

2. I could lead the spade jack from dummy and if East covers I could win and return to dummy with a club (running the risk of a ruff). I could then lead another spade and finesse the nine. This wins if East has K 10, K 10 2, K 10 4, or K 4 2 of spades. (This line has about 25½ percent chance of success if you ignore the risk of a club ruff. It has less chance, of course, if you take into consideration the possibility of a singleton club.)

3. I could lead the spade eight from the dummy to my queen. This wins if East has the K, K 4 2, K 4, K 2, or K 10 of spades. (This line adds up to almost a 33 percent chance of success and is clearly superior. By the way, nobody figures out exact percentages like that at the table. You figure those out later when somebody asks you why you played it a certain way.)

Did I adopt line 3 which is obviously best? No. I chose 2, which I knew had the least mathematical chance of success. Why? Because East looked too alert. According to my calculations East should have been in a very hopeless frame of mind after his partner cashed the ace of diamonds. He could see that any club finesse I might need would work, and with the doubleton king of trumps he should feel that his spade king was a goner. Yet he didn't look like a man who knew the jig was up. There could only be two explanations for his continued confidence in life: (1) He didn't have the spade king and was hoping his partner could win a trump trick, or (2) he had K 10 x or K 10 x x of trumps and expected to win the setting trick himself.

So I led the spade jack from dummy. East covered and I won with the ace, returned to the board with a club, discarded the diamond jack on the heart ace, and took another trump finesse. East's spade holding was K 10 4 and I made the slam.

Moral: One twitch of an opponent's eyebrow is worth two degrees in mathematics!

\*　　　\*　　　\*

The hands that appeal to me the most are those where a player "creates" a huge profit out of practically nothing. Here's an example from a rubber bridge game at the Cavendish club, where my partner, Al Roth, manufactured a tremendous swing in our favor just by listening to the opponents.

Both sides vulnerable:

                    NORTH
            ♠ Q 9 8 5 4 2
            ♡ K Q
            ◇ 10 3
            ♣ Q J 2

    WEST                            EAST
♠ J 10 7 3                      ♠ A K 6
♡ 5 4                           ♡ 9 7 6 3 2
◇ A Q J 6 2                     ◇ 8 4
♣ 7 6                           ♣ 5 4 3

                    SOUTH
            ♠ —
            ♡ A J 10 8
            ◇ K 9 7 5
            ♣ A K 10 9 8

The bidding:

| SOUTH | WEST | NORTH | EAST |
|-------|------|-------|------|
| 1 ♣ | Pass | 1 ♠ | Pass |
| 2 ♣ | Pass | 2 ♠ | Pass |
| 2 NT | Pass | 3 NT | Pass |
| Pass | Double | Pass | Pass |
| Pass | | | |

Roth was West and I was East. Roth doubled the final contract of three no-trump even though he had only eight points and a partner who had never bid. His reasoning was this. Both North and South had tried to sign off below game. Thus their total assets figured to come to slightly less than 26 points. As he himself had only eight points, I must have had the remainder. With the diamond suit banked over declarer, Roth could see a big profit if he could just find my entry.

After some thought he led the spade three. South expected Roth to have the high cards for his double so he played dummy's queen and I won with the king. Declarer didn't want to part with one of his nine winners, so he threw a diamond. I returned a diamond to West's jack and another spade lead put me in to lead my last diamond. We took the first nine tricks for a score of 1400. Very few players would even think of doubling with Roth's cards and most of them wouldn't have beaten three no-trump anyway.

\*　　　　\*　　　　\*

This last hand occurred many years ago at the New York Regency Club. The famous expert Charles Lochridge wrote it up in *Bridge World Magazine*, and although I am not personally involved I am including it because I think it is one of the funniest bridge stories I've ever read.

East dealer, neither vulnerable:

```
                    NORTH
                 ♠ 7 5 2
                 ♡ Q 6 5
                 ◇ 9 8 6 2
                 ♣ Q 7 4

   WEST                         EAST
♠ K Q J 8 6                  ♠ A 10 9 4 3
♡ J 10 8 3                   ♡ —
◇ 4 3                        ◇ 7
♣ J 5                        ♣ A K 10 9 8 3 2

                    SOUTH
                 ♠ —
                 ♡ A K 9 7 4 2
                 ◇ A K Q J 10 5
                 ♣ 6
```

The bidding:

| EAST | SOUTH | WEST | NORTH |
|------|-------|------|-------|
| 1 ♣ | Pass(!) | 1 ♠ | Pass |
| 3 ◇ (!) | Pass(!) | 3 ♠ | Pass |
| 4 ♠ | 6 ◇ | Double | Pass |
| Pass | Pass | | |

Lochridge was South, Ted Lightner was North, Mrs. S. Wainwright was East, and Sam Fry, Jr., was West.

According to Charlie, when he jumped to six diamonds, Sam Fry was so startled that he doubled without giving the situation a second thought. Lochridge's partner, the ever-lugubrious Lightner, gazed at Lochridge as though he had been stabbed in the back. The rest of the story should be told in Charlie's own words.

West opened the jack of clubs and when I got a look at the dummy I was so impressed with my own brilliance that I forgot to cover. When his jack held the trick Fry went into a coma.

How long this might have lasted there is no way of telling, but I could see that Lightner was suffering unbearably (and besides my own time at the bridge table is extremely valuable) so I spread my hand and claimed the balance. No one has ever accused Sam of being unable to count to thirteen! He shifted to a heart which his partner trumped.

I managed to grab Lightner before he jumped out the window, and tried to console him with the fact that the opponents could have made six spades. But even today, after all these years, every time Lightner sees me his mumbled greeting sounds suspiciously like "you big jerk."

# ABOUT THE AUTHOR

DOROTHY HAYDEN was born in New York City and attended Smith College and Western Michigan College. She taught mathematics and was an actuarial student with the New York Life Insurance Company. She is the mother of four children and now lives in Hastings-on-Hudson, New York.

Mrs. Hayden started her bridge career not as a player but, to quote her, as a "kibitzer." At the age of seven she discovered that she could play bridge and from that time on she was a bridge enthusiast.

One of the outstanding woman players of the world, Dorothy Hayden was the first woman to make the American International Bridge Team on the basis of competitive play. She also was the youngest member of the team. In May, 1965, she represented the United States against Great Britain, Argentina, and Italy.

Dorothy Hayden Truscott has won thirteen major national titles, and has represented the United States ten times in international competition. In 1974 and 1976 she was a member of American teams that defeated the European Women's champions in challenge matches for the Venice Trophy. She is the only American to have competed in all four forms of major international competition: open teams, open pairs, women's teams, and women's pairs. She is married to Alan Truscott, bridge editor of the New York Times.

# THE GAMES PEOPLE PLAY

☐ **41-054-9 WINNING BACKGAMMON**
**by Michael S. Lawrence** $2.50
Double your pleasure, double your skills...with this innovative do-it-yourself guide to backgammon—designed to help the beginner learn winning strategies.

☐ **41-316-5 PLAY OF THE HAND WITH BLACKWOOD**
**by Easley Blackwood (hardcover size)** $11.95
Here is the long-awaited, essential bridge book by one of the world's great masters—an indispensable guide for beginners and experts alike!

☐ **41-265-7 BID BETTER, PLAY BETTER: HOW TO THINK AT THE BRIDGE TABLE**
**by Dorothy Hayden Truscott** $2.50
Bridge-expert Dorothy Truscott gives tournament-tested advice on all vital bridge points in this straightforward, imaginative, and easy-to-follow guide.

**Buy them at your local bookstore or use this handy coupon.**
Clip and mail this page with your order

**PINNACLE BOOKS, INC.—Reader Service Dept.**
**271 Madison Ave., New York, NY 10016**

Please send me the book(s) I have checked above. I am enclosing $_____
(please add 75¢ to cover postage and handling). Send check or money order only—no cash or C.O.D.'s.

Mr./Mrs./Miss _____

Address _____

City_____ State/Zip_____

Please allow six weeks for delivery. Prices subject to change without notice.